The
Sentence of the Court
A Handbook for Magistrates

A basic outline of the law, practice and procedure of sentencing in magistrates' courts, produced under the auspices of the Justices' Clerks' Society for use by newly appointed justices of the peace and others concerned with the sentencing of offenders in summary proceedings.

SECOND EDITION

The
Sentence of the Court
A Handbook for Magistrates

SECOND EDITION

Published 1998 by
WATERSIDE PRESS
Domum Road
Winchester SO23 9NN
Telephone or Fax 01962 855567
INTERNET:106025.1020@compuserve.com

ISBN Paperback 1 872 870 64 3

Cataloguing-in-Publication Data A catalogue record for this book can be obtained from the British Library

Printing and binding Antony Rowe Ltd, Chippenham

Cover design John Good Holbrook Ltd, Coventry

The Sentence of the Court is also available in a loose-leaf format (A4) as part of the *Magistrates Bench Handbook* developed in partnership with the Judicial Studies Board, Magistrates' Association and Justices' Clerks' Society: Waterside Press, 1998, ISBN 1 872 870 62 7.

The
Sentence of the Court
A Handbook for Magistrates

Michael Watkins
Winston Gordon
Anthony Jeffries

Foreword by

Lord Bingham of Cornhill
Lord Chief Justice

Editor Bryan Gibson

Under the auspices of the
Justices' Clerks' Society

SECOND EDITION

WATERSIDE PRESS
WINCHESTER

The authors

Michael Watkins is Director of Legal Services and Joint Justices' Clerk for Warwickshire. He has contributed to training programmes for magistrates for the Judicial Studies Board and at the Universities of Birmingham and Cambridge. He is a member of the Executive Committee of the Justices' Clerks' Society Standing Committee of Magistrates' Training Officers. He is a solicitor, a member of the Society's Criminal Law Network and co-author of *Introduction to the Youth Court*.

Winston Gordon is Justices' Clerk, Justices' Chief Executive and Training Officer for Tameside, Greater Manchester. He is a member of the Executive Committee of the Justices' Clerks' Society Standing Committee of Magistrates' Training Officers and of the Duchy of Lancaster Branch Training Committee. He is a solicitor—with experience of advocacy—a tutor at Continuing Professional Development courses and co-author of *Introduction to the Youth Court* and *Introduction to the Family Proceedings Court*.

Anthony Jeffries is Justices' Clerk and Justices' Chief Executive for Birmingham and Sutton Coldfield and a member of the Executive Committee of the Justices' Clerks' Society Standing Committee of Magistrates' Training Officers. He is a barrister and a member of the Advisory Group for Magistrates' Courses, Board of Continuing Education, University of Cambridge.

Editor

Bryan Gibson is Managing Editor of Waterside Press.

The
Sentence of the Court
A Handbook for Magistrates

SECOND EDITION

Contents

Appendices

*Reproduced by kind permission of the Magistrates' Association

This handbook deals with *adult* offenders, ie those aged 18 years and over. Younger offenders normally appear in the youth court where they are sentenced by specially trained magistrates: see, generally, *Introduction to the Youth Court*. Exceptionally, offenders below the age of 18 may be sentenced in the ordinary magistrates' court (eg when the case also involves an adult). This handbook deals with the sentencing of people under 18 years of age only to this extent: see *Appendix F*. At the time of writing it is believed that consideration is being given to legislation which would return 17 year olds to the adult court.

Foreword

Deciding the appropriate level of sentence is one of the most difficult tasks which magistrates have to perform. They must, within the limits set by Parliament, have regard to the seriousness of the offence, the circumstances of the offender, the effect of the offence on the victim and the public interest in restraining criminal conduct. They must not be too rigid in their approach, so as to treat different cases as if they were alike; but they must not allow levels of sentence to be, or appear to be, arbitrary and inconsistent. It is a task calling for the exercise of a very careful judgment.

This handbook produced under the auspices of the Justices' Clerks' Society, and now in a welcome second edition, will not solve all the problems which arise. But it will prove invaluable to magistrates seeking to approach their sentencing task in a just and principled way. I hope it will command the wide readership it deserves.

Bingham, C. J.

Aims and Objectives

The Sentence of the Court was compiled under the auspices of the Justices' Clerks' Society by three experienced training officers to magistrates. The aims are:

- to provide a companion for new magistrates as they undertake their basic training and come new to the task of sentencing

- to assist trainers by allowing them to concentrate on imparting skills necessary for making informed, balanced and structured sentence decisions—in the knowledge that background material can be found in the handbook

- to provide an accessible reference point for magistrates generally

- to inform other court users and students about how sentence decisions are approached in magistrates' courts; and

- to produce a lucid account, avoiding jargon and complexity. Statutory and other references—the province of court legal/judicial advisers and other lawyers—are not reproduced unless particularly significant or where they are in everyday use.

Important note

The information contained in *The Sentence of the Court* cannot replace legal/judicial advice, which should be sought *in all but the most straightforward cases:* see, particularly, *Chapter 11.*

Within the text, a 'helping hand' symbol serves to indicate complex areas of law where magistrates should proceed with extra caution and seek further explanation/advice locally.

The 'helping hand' symbol is as follows: 📖✋

Chapter 1

Introduction

Virtually all criminal prosecutions—ranging from those for the simplest parking offences to the most heinous murders—start out in the magistrates' court. Unless cases are withdrawn, or discontinued by the prosecutor, around 97 per cent are dealt with to their final conclusion by magistrates, either by acquittal or conviction and sentence. Conviction stems from a plea of 'guilty' or from a finding of guilt—based on the evidence in the case—where someone has pleaded 'not guilty'. Over 1.3 million cases a year are sentenced by magistrates. The remaining cases are dealt with by the Crown Court, having been sent there by magistrates' courts: for trial by jury; for sentence; or to be dealt with: see *Chapter 2*.

JURISDICTION

The sentencing powers of magistrates are laid down by Acts of Parliament. Jurisdiction to deal with cases and, in many instances, the maximum sentence available depends on the legal status of the offence charged. There are two main classifications (the first of which is divided into two sub-categories):

Indictable offences

(i) Indictable only
Purely indictable offences can only be dealt with by the Crown Court. Examples are: murder (which carries a mandatory life-sentence), rape, robbery, serious firearms offences and wounding with intent to do grievous bodily harm. These offences are brought before a magistrates' court initially, but must then be sent to the Crown Court for trial before a judge and jury. The Crime and Disorder Bill (1997) proposes the abolition of committal proceedings for indictable only offences so that magistrates will in future commit such cases forthwith to the Crown Court for trial.

(ii) Either way offences
Either way offences can be tried by magistrates (ie 'summarily') or by the Crown Court (ie 'on indictment'). The decision as to the venue for trial and/or sentence is now, since 1 October 1997, subject to revised

9

procedures which are dealt with in *Chapter 2*. Common examples of either way offences are: theft, criminal damage, assault occasioning actual bodily harm, most of the more serious drugs offences and burglary (provided that this last offence is not 'aggravated', eg involving the use of a weapon—when it becomes indictable only).

Where either way cases *are* heard by magistrates their sentencing powers are generally limited to six months imprisonment and/or a fine of £5,000 per offence—plus any ancillary orders (such as compensation or disqualification) which are appropriate. Sentences of imprisonment may be made concurrent to one another, or possibly consecutive: see *Chapter 3*. Where consecutive sentences are passed by magistrates for two or more either way offences their maximum powers are normally 12 months in aggregate.

The Crown Court usually has power to pass a longer sentence for an either way offence than the magistrates' court does (eg theft: up to seven years; criminal damage: up to ten years). Whenever magistrates are in a position to sentence for an either way offence there is power to commit to the Crown Court for sentence if they feel that the greater sentencing powers of the Crown Court should be invoked: *Chapter 2*.

Summary offences

In the normal course of events, summary offences can only be tried and sentences for them can only be passed by a magistrates' court. Examples of purely summary offences are: most road traffic offences (*Chapter 7*), the less serious public order offences, having 'no television licence' and contravening local bye-laws. The magistrates deal with the entire case: taking a plea, deciding upon guilt or innocence and—in the event of conviction—the sentence. Only in limited circumstances can summary offences be sent to the Crown Court for trial or sentence (eg where the summary matter is interwoven with other matters which can be sent to the Crown Court for trial or sentence).

The maximum sentence for a summary offence is fixed by the statute which creates the offence, usually by reference to one of five fining levels (*Chapter 3*) and in some instances imprisonment of one, two, three or six months.

BACKGROUND TO CURRENT PRACTICE

The Criminal Justice Act 1991 made significant changes to the way in which the sentencing of offenders is approached. The criteria set out in that Act serve as a framework for present day sentencing practice. An underlying aim was to ensure that sentences are proportionate to the seriousness of the offence or offences of which an offender stands convicted. The 1991 Act uses the term 'commensurate' to describe such sentences—and at the time of the legislation the government called this a 'just deserts' approach. Principal features of the Act (which has been significantly amended on a number of occasions since 1991) are:

A framework for sentencing
A legal framework was created within which there are statutory criteria for the use of fines, community sentences and custody. In effect, the facts of a case—ie information about the offence itself—must be considered alongside these criteria. The framework is explained in *Chapter 3* of this handbook, which identifies four levels of sentence as follows:

- discharges
- fines
- community sentences; and
- custody.

When passing sentence, a court must decide upon

- the appropriate level of sentence within the framework based on the seriousness of the offence; and
- the extent of the chosen sentence within that level, again based on the seriousness of the offence (eg the *size* of a fine, the total *number of hours* community service, the *length* of a prison sentence).

Seriousness
The 1991 Act made the seriousness of the offence itself the main initial focus of sentence decision-making. Assessing seriousness involves:

- forming a view about the general level of seriousness of an offence. To bring about consistency of approach, each bench has its own local guidelines, or it may follow the Magistrates' Association *Sentencing Guidelines* (reproduced as *Appendix C* to this handbook) or a variant of these;
- then looking at the facts of the individual offence and considering aggravating factors (ie which make the offence *more* serious than other offences of its type) and mitigating factors (which make it *less so*). Examples of seriousness factors are contained in *Chapter 2*. An offence committed whilst the offender is already on bail must, by law, be treated as more serious by virtue of that fact.

The *personal circumstances* of the offender may occasionally affect the seriousness of the offence, but they are normally taken into account later in the sentencing process (see page 22) or as part of the offender's personal (or 'offender') mitigation (page 31). The normal steps are summarised in *A Structured Guide to Sentencing* on pages 66 and 67.

Fines

The 1991 Act introduced a short-lived system of 'unit fines' under which courts related the seriousness of an offence to a number of units on a scale from one to 50, then multiplied that number by the offender's 'disposable weekly income'. The Criminal Justice Act 1993 substituted a less mathematical and more flexible arrangement within which the size of the fine must, nevertheless, still reflect both the seriousness of the offence and the offender's financial circumstances. The unit fines system had the effect of increasing the amount of the fine according to the offender's financial circumstances and the 1993 Act, on repealing that system, retained this aspect by giving the court the express power to increase as well as decrease a fine according to such circumstances. It also re-enacted in a new form a power to order the offender to provide details to the court of his or her finances (known as a 'financial circumstances order'). Courts must take such information into account when available: see generally *Chapter 3*.

A number of courts have continued to operate a (non-statutory) unit approach—as to which it is necessary to seek details locally.

Community sentences

The description 'community sentence', introduced in 1991, is an all-embracing term for the six types of community order discussed in *Chapter 3* of this handbook, ie:

- probation order (with or without added requirements)
- community service order
- combination order*
- attendance centre order (under 21 years of age only)
- curfew order*
- supervision order (under 18s only).

The items marked with an asterisk were novel at the time of the 1991 Act—and the curfew order has still to be brought into force nationally (trials have taken place in an increasing number of areas of the country since July 1995).

Community orders are *sentences* in their own right. Even the probation order has become a sentence (it was originally an order 'in lieu of sentence'). It was also common before 1991 to hear the more severe forms of community order described as 'alternatives to custody'. Strictly speaking, the only remaining true alternative to custody is now a special form of supervision for offenders below 18 years of age (and it is proposed that this will be changed in the Crime and Disorder Bill (1997)). 📖✋

The 'serious enough' test

A threshold was created whereby an offence must be 'serious enough' to merit a community sentence before any of the six community orders can be used—usually called the 'serious enough' test.

Restriction on liberty

The 1991 Act established a new impetus in favour of community based sentences, which were intended to restrict the liberty of the offender without the need to resort to a custodial sentence. It thus introduced the notion of 'restriction on liberty'. The restriction created by the order must be commensurate with the seriousness of the offence. Thus eg a probation order containing a requirement that the offender attend at a probation centre and take part in a programme intended to confront, say, alcohol or drug abuse, restricts liberty to the extent that whilst attending the centre the offender is not free to do other things—whilst the demands made by the programme itself (which may involve substantial changes in the offender's lifestyle) cannot be discounted. Even a basic probation order will make considerable demands on the time and energies of the offender. Similarly, community service restricts liberty whilst the offender is doing unpaid work in the community.

Suitability

When passing a community sentence, the court must select the order (or orders) which is (or are) most suitable for the particular offender. Suitability thus has to be balanced with the restriction on liberty demanded by the seriousness of the offence.

Cumulative orders

The 1991 Act made it possible, in theory, for community orders to be made cumulatively—ie in addition to one another—provided that the seriousness of the offence justifies this. Great care must be exercised in relation to cumulative orders so that the overall sentence does not become *disproportionate*. There may also be technical or practical considerations and magistrates are urged to seek legal advice if considering such a course of action. 📖✋

Probation and community service can only be combined in a combination order: see *Chapter 3*. Opinions differ as to whether a fine may also be added to a community order for a single offence. 📖✋

Custody

At the top of the sentencing framework is custody. For adult offenders, custody means:

- imprisonment in the case of an offender aged 21 or over
- detention in a young offender institution in the case of someone below 21 years of age.

The 1991 Act introduced three initial bases for custody. The first of these is, by far, the one most commonly applied in the magistrates' court:

- *The 'so serious' test*

In practice, custody is reserved primarily for situations where the offence is of such a level of seriousness that all other types of sentence are ruled out. The threshold test for custody requires the court to be of the opinion that the offence is so serious that *only* such a sentence can be justified—often called the 'so serious' test.

- *The 'protection of the public' test*

In relation to custodial sentences for sexual or violent offences (see pages 60 and 61), the 1991 Act also introduced, by way of an alternative to the so serious test above, the need to protect the public from serious harm from the offender in question. This may justify a custodial sentence irrespective of the seriousness of the offence. It may also justify a longer sentence (within the legal maximum). Where the protection of the public from serious harm *is* in the court's mind, there will often be sound reasons to consider committing to the Crown Court for sentence.

- *Custody on refusal of a community sentence*

Custody can sometimes be used even though neither the 'so serious' test nor the 'protection of the public' test is satisfied. This is where a community sentence is proposed by the court and the offender refuses to consent to it. But this only applies where consent is a legal pre-requisite. The Crime (Sentences) Act 1997 has, with effect from 1 October 1997, significantly reduced the circumstances where consent to a community order is required: see, generally, under *Community Sentences* in *Chapter 3*. Similarly, custody can be used (where the offence is itself imprisonable) if an offender wilfully and persistently fails to comply with a community order once made.

All the above points are expanded on in *Chapter 3*.

Suspended sentences
Once imprisonment has been decided upon—but not before—it can be suspended for one to two years (although *not* detention in a young offender institution). The rule, since the 1991 Act, is that there must be 'exceptional circumstances' to justify the suspension: *Chapter 3.*

Reasons for decisions
The 1991 Act (and subsequent legislation) has added to the situations in which magistrates are obliged to announce reasons for sentence-related decisions and these are noted at appropriate points in later chapters. Judicial decisions must always be based on sound reasoning, whether needing to be announced or not. This is why a structured approach to decision-making—as recommended by the Judicial Studies Board—is advisable. It ensures that all relevant matters are taken into account, weighed and considered.

Early release
The 1991 Act introduced a new scheme of early release from prison (and from detention in a young offender institution)—a purpose being to create greater certainty about the proportion of time actually served under custodial sentences. These provisions are complex and have been subject to review. 📖✋
      Magistrates acquired important responsibilities to deal with breach of licence and to return offenders to prison if they commit a fresh imprisonable offence whilst on release: see *Chapter 9.*

Enforcement
A feature of the 1991 Act was an improvement in powers and procedures relating to enforcement of sentences. Firm powers allow, eg for re-sentencing on breach of a community order. If the breach is deemed by the court to be wilful and persistent the court can treat this as tantamount to a refusal to consent to one of those few community orders which requires consent—which is another basis for a custodial sentence: see above and *Chapter 3.* As already indicated, the early release provisions mentioned under the last heading allow magistrates to send or return offenders to custody.

'Section 95'
Sentencers have traditionally argued that a court should not be prevented from passing a given sentence merely because of its cost. Without attempting to introduce cost controls, section 95 Criminal Justice Act 1991 places a duty on the home secretary to inform sentencers of the '. . . financial implications of their decisions . . .'. This same provision requires the Home Secretary to provide information to

courts and others about discrimination generally. This is dealt with in *Appendix E, Equality of Treatment and Section 95.*

OTHER KEY DEVELOPMENTS

Since 1991, there have been other key developments, including:

Associated offences
The original 1991 Act restriction on considering only one associated offence has now been removed, thereby permitting all such offences to be considered when assessing seriousness. Offences are 'associated' offences (📖✋) if they are:

- offences of which the offender has been convicted in the same proceedings; or
- offences of which the offender has been convicted in other proceedings (by the same or another court) and which have now been referred to the present court for sentencing; or
- offences to be taken into consideration (TICs).

> **References throughout this handbook to the seriousness of an offence should be understood to mean the offence and any associated offences which are relevant when assessing seriousness.**

Earlier convictions and responses
All previous convictions and responses to earlier sentences can now, if considered relevant, be taken into account when assessing the seriousness of the present offence. However, great care is needed when deciding how to apply the governing statutory provision, section 29 Criminal Justice Act 1991. This is the subject matter of *Chapter 6.*

Pre-sentence reports
The 1991 Act introduced the pre-sentence report or 'PSR'. So far as magistrates' courts are concerned, the underlying rule is that a PSR must be obtained *before*:

- deciding whether an offence is so serious that only a custodial sentence is justified and how long that sentence should be;
- deciding, in the case of a violent or sexual offence, whether a custodial sentence is necessary to protect the public from serious harm from the offender or whether a longer sentence should for that reason be passed than is indicated by the seriousness of the offence;

- making certain community orders (and, in particular, before considering whether they are suitable for an offender).

Although these obligations to obtain a PSR remain, courts can, if they consider it appropriate, as a result of the Criminal Justice and Public Order Act 1994, deem such a report to be 'unnecessary'. Pre-sentence reports are governed by a Home Office 'National Standard for Pre-sentence Reports' and are the subject matter of *Chapter 8.*

Credit for a guilty plea

It had long been the practice in the Crown Court, and in those criminal courts above it, to consider reducing a sentence in appropriate cases where the defendant had entered a timely guilty plea. This practice had started to find its way into magistrates' courts, although the scope for substantial reduction was probably more limited because of the different types of cases dealt with by magistrates. The practice was put on a statutory footing for all criminal courts by the Criminal Justice and Public Order Act 1994. Thus courts are now required to consider the possibility of giving credit for a guilty plea based on both

- the stage in the proceedings when the guilty plea occurred; and
- the circumstances in which it was entered.

It is likely that courts will find the pre-1994 case law relevant to the statutory provisions. Thus credit will reflect factors such as

- true remorse and contrition
- saving witnesses the ordeal of giving evidence (especially in sexual cases, although the 'protection of the public' consideration will also apply: *see above*)
- assisting the police with their enquiries and for example helping to recover stolen goods
- saving public funds and resources by pleading guilty.

Many courts now, following case law, adopt a 'graded' approach to giving credit for a guilty plea. The 1997 version of *the Magistrates' Association Sentencing Guidelines* (see *Appendix C* to this handbook) recognises this practice. The credit could therefore start at 'no credit at all' where the offender has been caught red-handed committing a serious offence and has no real option but to plead guilty (a case more often perhaps found in the Crown Court). At the maximum the credit could be as much as one third where the offender has really gone out of his or her way to co-operate and make amends. Most magistrates' courts will give at least some minimum credit for a timely guilty plea just to encourage defendants to reduce the pressures on the court system.

Where the offence is an either way offence, credit for a guilty plea is one of the factors to be considered when magistrates are deciding whether to sentence an offender themselves or to commit to the Crown Court for sentence: see *Appendix B*.

Where credit *is* given the court must announce that fact (but not necessarily the extent of the credit given). This is usually recorded on the court file and in the court register. Many courts informally announce if they have *not* given credit for a guilty plea, to inform the offender and other people, and to make matters clearer if there is an appeal.

Credit for a guilty plea is, of itself, unlikely ever to result in the reduction of the level of sentence, eg from custody to a community order. Equally, case law suggests that someone who pleads guilty will not usually receive the absolute maximum sentence for that offence.

Concerning this topic, it is wise to take further advice locally: 📖✋

SENTENCING IN CONTEXT

The next two chapters place the modern developments outlined in this chapter into context. *Chapter 2* deals with certain broad procedural considerations as well as with some further general factors which affect all sentencing decisions, whilst *Chapter 3* looks in greater detail at the sentencing framework and the range of sentences available.

APPEALS AND RE-OPENING OF DECISIONS

People convicted and sentenced by a magistrates' court can appeal to the Crown Court against their conviction, their sentence, or both—or to the High Court on a point of law. In limited circumstances, magistrates can themselves re-open the matter. For an outline, see *Appendix G*.

To appeal to the Crown Court (the usual method, especially in sentencing matters), the offender must give written notice within 21 days, setting out the general grounds of appeal. The case of *R v Swindon Crown Court, ex parte Murray, The Times,* 24 September 1997, confirmed that when hearing an appeal the Crown Court must approach sentencing afresh and form its own independent view. Often, it will have later information and the fact that it may impose a different sentence does not of itself suggest that the magistrates were wrong in principle. The sentence imposed by the Crown Court may be less severe or more severe—but limited to magistrates' maximum powers of punishment.

Chapter 2

General Considerations

As outlined in *Chapter 1*, sentence decisions are made within a statutory sentencing framework—the central rule being that a sentence should be commensurate with the seriousness of the offence. The framework can be viewed as comprising the following:

- Four levels of sentence (see *Chapter 3*)
- Statutory criteria whereby, for the greater part, the seriousness of the offence determines the level within which the sentence should be fixed—and the extent of the sentence within that level
- Special considerations which attach to most sexual or violent offences, and which may lead to a custodial sentence—or a longer custodial sentence than would be justified simply by the seriousness of the offence—if necessary to protect the public from serious harm from the offender
- Provisions which require courts to consider relevant information (including, when appropriate, a pre-sentence report ('PSR')) and to adopt other procedures when passing sentence.

These items must be set against the wider background to sentencing law and practice as it has developed over the years—and within which there are certain 'general objects of sentencing'.

GENERAL OBJECTS OF SENTENCING

Historically, there have been six traditionally recognised objects of sentencing for courts to try and achieve. These are:

- punishment/retribution
- reparation (including financial compensation to a victim)
- protection of the public
- deterrence
- reflecting proper public concern
- rehabilitation.

To these objects might be added a further aim: that of 'disposal', ie each offence requires its own sentence. On occasion, a minor form of sentence (a nominal fine or absolute discharge) may be appropriate simply to dispose of the matter. Also, the non-statutory practice of imposing 'no separate penalty' (NSP) has developed. This allows the court—usually in the case of multiple offences—to deal with lesser matters without adding to the total sentence once the offender has been sentenced for the most serious offences at an appropriate level.

When 'proportionate', 'commensurate' and 'just desserts' principles were invoked via the Criminal Justice Act 1991 (*Chapter 1*) there was uncertainty as to whether—or to what extent—such sentencing objects had survived. In 1997, Lord Bingham of Cornhill, Lord Chief Justice, explored traditional sentencing objects in a speech to the Police Foundation.[1] The following main points emerge.

Punishment/retribution
It is fundamental to the idea of 'just deserts' that sentences contain an appropriate, ie a commensurate, level of punishment.

Reparation
Making reparation, ie putting something back by way of acts intended to benefit the victim or the community is an underlying rationale of community sentences, particularly community service. The fact eg that an offender has made voluntary reparation may indicate remorse or contrition and thereby, depending on the circumstances, justify some reduction of sentence (see also *Credit for a guilty* plea in *Chapter 1*). Compensation to victims of crime is one aspect of reparation and a constant sentencing consideration. This is considered in *Chapter 4*.

Protection of the public
Lord Bingham also called this aspect 'incapacitation', ie while serving a custodial sentence the offender is unable for the period in question to inflict more offending on the public. Protection of the public has emerged in a clearer, more defined way in the special custody provisions affecting most sexual or violent offences: see *Chapter 3*. In relation to other types of offence, the need to protect the public may be a relevant consideration but will not permit any sentence in excess of what is commensurate with the seriousness of the offence.

Deterrence
In one of the first cases to come before the Court of Appeal following the 1991 Act, the previous Lord Chief Justice, Lord Taylor, sought to clarify whether deterrent sentences were consistent with proportionality in sentencing. His conclusions can be summarised as follows:

- custodial sentences in particular are meant to punish *and* deter
- the deterrence will affect both the offender and other people

---

[1] Lord Bingham's address is reported in full in *Justice of the Peace and Local Government Law*, 150 JPN 700, 19 July 1997.

- such a sentence—in having to be commensurate with the seriousness of the offence—had to be commensurate with the punishment and deterrence which the seriousness of the offence required (*R v Cunningham* (1993) 14 Cr. App. R. (S.) 386).

However, the Court of Appeal made it clear that *increasing* a sentence beyond the length which by those criteria is commensurate with seriousness to make an example of the defendant (an 'exemplary sentence') offends the principle of proportionality.

Reflecting proper public concern
The Court of Appeal has retained, certainly so far as custodial sentences are concerned, the concept of a right thinking member of the public in possession of all the facts feeling that in certain cases justice cannot be done without a custodial sentence being passed: *R v Cox (David Geoffrey)* (1993) 14 Cr. App. R. (S.) 619.

Rehabilitation
Rehabilitation has found a new place due to the emphasis on the suitability for the offender of community orders—and expressly as one of the statutory purposes of probation: *Chapter 3*. It is also an underlying rationale of *The Early Release Scheme: Chapter 9*.

THE TOTALITY PRINCIPLE

Where there are a number of offences, the sentences, in combination, should not be out of all proportion to the nature of the overall offending under consideration. What the totality principle means in practice is that when imposing several sentences at the same time—particularly if they concern the same events—magistrates should review the total effect and make such downward adjustments as are appropriate.

STRUCTURED DECISION-MAKING

The Judicial Studies Board has encouraged courts to make decisions by reference to a structure which can be represented by way of a chart or series of questions. An example appears on pages 66-7. Central to this in relation to the sentencing process is an assessment of the seriousness of the offence to ensure that the sentence relates primarily to the offence itself and is proportionate to it. This involves deciding:

- how serious it is in general terms. Some offences (eg burglary) are inherently more serious than others (eg theft). This gives a starting point within the sentencing framework; and

- what other, more individual and offence-based factors in the present case affect the initial assessment of the level of seriousness for this type of offence—often called 'aggravating' and 'mitigating' factors.

A main task is to weigh these latter factors to see whether, and to what extent, the offence is more or less serious than the general run of comparable cases. The Magistrates' Association *Sentencing Guidelines* (see *Appendix C* to this handbook) begin by asking whether a particular level of sentence is appropriate. They then list specific ingredients which might make the offence more or less serious. The main purpose of guidelines is to encourage consistency of approach. The following is a general list of the kind of *offence* based factors which may fall to be taken into account:

—type of offence
—use or threat of violence
—use of or carrying of weapon
—value of any property stolen or damaged
—extent of any injuries
—presence of racial motive
—vulnerability of victim
—offence against public servant acting as such
—abuse of trust or power
—premeditated as opposed to 'spur of the moment'
—prime mover as opposed to minor participant
—adult using children in commission of the offence
—time and place of the offence
—involvement of drink or drugs
—offence on bail
—immediate remorse or concern for victim such as might be shown immediately at the time of the offence (eg by calling an ambulance after an assault)
—offence of need as opposed to greed
—provocation.

Additionally, certain *offender* based factors may affect the court's view of the seriousness of the offence eg: age, maturity, intelligence, health. However, these factors—along with such items as an early guilty plea or the offender's attitude to the offence (either of which may indicate remorse or contrition), efforts aimed at reparation to the victim, or co-operation with the police—are more typically viewed as 'personal mitigation': see under *Sentencing Information* below. The defendant's earlier convictions and responses to sentences can affect the seriousness of the current offence—but great care is needed when applying this rule: see *Chapter 6.*

Offences committed whilst on bail

By statute, a court is obliged to treat an offence committed on bail as more serious by virtue of that fact. The relevant provision reads:

> In considering the seriousness of any offence committed while the offender was on bail, the court shall treat the fact that it was committed in those circumstances as an aggravating factor.

Despite the apparent strictness of this requirement, during the relevant Parliamentary debate, a spokesman indicated that:

> The Government do not intend that an offence committed on bail will always lead to a longer sentence. That would be absurd where the two offences are totally unconnected, or the second offence is a trivial one . . .

Prevalence of offences

The fact that an offence is prevalent may make it more serious. This may be within a particular locality. A distinction must be drawn between the fact that an offence occurs frequently (the usual starting point for sentencing should already reflect this) and what might be termed 'a real outburst' of a particular type of offence and one that is perhaps gaining momentum. Court of Appeal guidance gives examples of ways in which the prevalence of an offence can increase its seriousness: eg a spate of sexual attacks on women can increase fear among women generally in an area and limit their freedom of movement. The decision as to what effect prevalence has is ultimately for the court *in all the circumstances.*

THE SENTENCING PROCESS OUTLINED

The trial and sentencing process depends on the category of the offence. These categories (ie 'indictable only', 'either way' and 'summary') are explained in *Chapter 1.*

Indictable only offences

The Crime and Disorder Bill (1997) proposes that indictable only cases are committed forthwith to the Crown Court. At the time of writing, they start before the magistrates' court which deals with preliminary matters such as remands and legal aid. From the outset, the magistrates sit as 'examining justices' with a view to committing the case to the Crown Court for trial by jury. Trial and sentence are reserved to that court.

Summary offences

In summary cases the magistrates proceed directly to the question of guilt or innocence by asking the defendant, as soon as possible, whether he or she pleads 'guilty' or 'not guilty'. Following a guilty plea or, alternatively, if the defendant is convicted after the court hears the evidence, the magistrates proceed to sentence the offender. They thus deal with the entire process. (Exceptionally, summary matters can accompany other classes of offence to the Crown Court: 📖✋)

Either way offences—'Plea before Venue'

Section 49 Criminal Procedure and Investigations Act 1996 (together with certain provisions of the Crime (Sentences) Act 1997) has, since 1 October 1997, radically altered the procedure for processing, and if needs be sentencing, in relation to either way offences (including 'small value' criminal damage charges). 📖✋ Section 49 confronts:

- the cost and delay of sending either way offences to the Crown Court for trial when they merely result in a guilty plea
- the fact that, historically, a large proportion of either way offences committed to the Crown Court for trial are sentenced within the powers available to magistrates

and places increased emphasis on encouraging defendants to seek sentencing credit for a timely guilty plea: *Chapter 1.*

The new procedure—generally known as 'plea before venue'—is simple in concept but not without problems of interpretation. 📖✋

When a defendant appears in respect of an either way offence:

- he or she should be invited to indicate as soon as possible what plea would be entered if the matter were to come to trial (be that before the magistrates or before the Crown Court)
- if a *guilty plea* is indicated, the magistrates, in essence, deem there to have been a formal guilty plea on summary trial and move directly to consider the appropriate sentence
- the magistrates then either:
  —sentence the offender themselves; or
  —commit the offender to the Crown Court for sentence (on bail or in custody: see page 36)
- if a *not guilty* plea is indicated or the defendant refuses or fails to indicate any plea then the standard 'mode of trial' procedures outlined below must be followed.

It can be readily appreciated that certain issues arise in relation to the 'plea before venue' procedure, eg:

- the Crown prosecutor (or other prosecutor) will need a detailed and full file for the first hearing so that, eg the charges can be finalised ready for the procedure to take place
- the defendant will need to be able to seek legal advice as soon as possible and will, in any event, need to have the procedure explained simply but carefully by the court
- he or she is clearly being encouraged to seek maximum credit through an early guilty plea, possibly foregoing his or her usual right to advance disclosure of the prosecution case (see under next sub-heading). An indication of guilt without knowledge of the strength of the prosecution case might be viewed as being 'straight from the heart': true remorse
- magistrates will, more than ever, need to be clear as to when custody is appropriate, and how long such a sentence should be.

Appendix B to this handbook, *Considerations Affecting Decisions Whether or Not to Commit to the Crown Court for Sentence,* gives guidance about the use and length of custody. The Justices' Clerks' Society has issued advice concerning credit for a guilty plea: see page 35. 📖✋

Either way offences—'Mode of Trial'
Where the defendant, following an invitation to indicate a plea says that it is 'not guilty' or refuses or fails to indicate a plea then the standard—and pre-existing—'mode of trial' procedure must be followed. This involves the magistrates in considering:

- the nature of the case
- whether the circumstances make it one of a serious character
- whether their own sentencing powers are likely to be adequate (usually up to six months imprisonment and/or a fine of up to £5,000 per offence; with the possibility of an aggregate period of imprisonment of 12 months: *Chapter 3*)
- any other circumstances which appear to make trial at the Crown Court or the magistrates' court more appropriate.

The magistrates must then decide whether they are prepared, subject to the defendant's consent, to hear the case themselves or whether to commit the defendant to the Crown Court for trial. In order for the court to arrive at this decision:

- the prosecutor's version of the facts has—for the time being—to be taken as correct (ie a 'worst case sentencing scenario')
- the prosecutor and then the defendant will make representations as to the venue for trial

- the court may (and indeed generally should) make full enquiry as to the circumstances of the allegations (but NB not of the defendant's previous record, mitigation or personal circumstances).

The court may then direct trial at the Crown Court or declare the matter suitable for summary trial (ie before magistrates). If summary trial *is* found to be appropriate by the magistrates then they must still obtain the defendant's free and informed consent before they can proceed to deal with the case themselves. The defendant must also be informed that if he or she *does* agree to summary trial and pleads guilty or is found guilty then the magistrates can still commit to the Crown Court for sentence: page 34. If consent *is* given the magistrates proceed to take the defendant's plea. If it is *not* forthcoming the case will proceed with a view to committal for trial in the Crown Court.

The *National Mode of Trial Guidelines* are reproduced in *Appendix A* to this handbook. These were issued in 1995 (and have not been amended to take account of the new section 49 'plea before venue' provisions). These should be referred to in all either way cases where mode of trial falls to be determined by magistrates; and may also be relevant as background to decisions to commit to the Crown Court for sentence: see the commentary to *Appendix B.* 📖✋

SENTENCING BY MAGISTRATES

Sentencing by magistrates only starts when one of the following events occurs:

- the defendant enters an unequivocal plea of guilty to a summary offence or is convicted following a contested hearing
- the defendant indicates an unequivocal plea of guilty to an either way offence under the new section 49 procedure
- following the mode of trial procedure for an either way offence, the magistrates accept summary jurisdiction, the defendant consents thereto and then enters an unequivocal plea of guilty or is convicted following a contested hearing.

Any question as to whether or not the defendant's plea or indication of plea is equivocal (ie when it is not really clear whether it is a true plea of guilty) must be addressed straightaway. If a difficulty remains or the court has any remaining doubts, the defendant should be invited to take legal advice. Where necessary, the plea should be treated as one of not guilty. 📖✋

The facts of the case

The court must sentence on the agreed or proved facts and any other relevant information such as the contents of a pre-sentence report (PSR) (*Chapter 8*) and plea in mitigation. Problems can occur in the following circumstances:

- *Guilty plea—facts contested*

The defendant pleads guilty but maintains that the facts—though supporting the offence charged—are substantially different to those alleged by the prosecutor, eg in an assault case both punching and kicking may be alleged whereas the defendant may strongly deny using his or her feet. Unless the prosecutor invites the court to proceed on the basis of the defendant's version, the court must usually hold a 'trial within a trial' to determine the true facts. This is known as a 'Newton hearing' (after *R v Newton* (1983) Cr. App. Rep. 13). The court must make a determination on the disputed facts, and should announce and record its finding. The case then proceeds on the basis of the facts found. 📖✋

- *Conviction on a different basis*

Following a not guilty plea, the court finds the case proved but not on the precise basis alleged by the prosecutor (eg the court may find that the defendant stole three items and not the ten alleged). Here, the court will convict on the basis of three items and announce and record this. There are also cases, mainly in respect of road traffic offences, where a court hearing a not guilty plea is empowered, of its own volition, to convict of a different and lesser charge (eg dangerous driving reduced to driving without due care and attention). Again, an announcement should be made so that the basis for sentencing is clear.

- *Self-defence*

There are cases of assault when the defence is one of self-defence and where it is for the prosecutor to disprove matters once properly raised by the defendant. If the case is nonetheless found proved it is essential for the court to announce, on convicting the defendant, whether it totally discounts any suggestion of self-defence or whether it accepts that there was a need for some force but that it feels the defendant over-reacted.

Credit for a guilty plea

The principles affecting credit for a guilty plea were outlined in *Chapter 1* (see page 17). It is important for courts to be clear as to when credit for a guilty plea will be given—or, indeed, will not be given (including in plea before venue situations pursuant to the section 49 procedures outlined above). It is important to know *what credit* will be given and *what announcement* will be made. Courts should never add a 'sentencing premium' so as to *increase* sentence because of a not guilty plea (or late plea of guilty). Rather, it is a question of whether credit should be lost.

Informants

Occasionally an offender will, on pleading guilty and trying to show remorse, seek to obtain sentencing credit by reference to help given to the police as an informer. Although giving offenders credit for doing what might be regarded as a public duty may seem unpalatable, the Court of Appeal has recognised the reality that much serious crime is prevented or detected only with the help of informants. Indeed, many such informants may have received cash incentives from the police, or have been involved in criminal activity themselves.

The submission of such items to the court is a delicate matter and usually involves the receipt by the court of a confidential note, commonly called a 'text'. Such matters require careful consideration and legal/judicial advice is essential. The Justices' Clerks' Society issued advice on texts in *JCS News Sheet* No. 97/45 of 1997. 📖✋

SENTENCING INFORMATION

The prosecutor will present the facts fairly and objectively, but will not enter the sentencing arena save in limited ways eg by:

- providing details of any criminal record and 'antecedents'
- challenging information which conflicts with that on the prosecution file
- where the court has a duty to make obligatory orders such as endorsement or disqualification, by reminding the court of this or countering suggestions by the defence that the court should refrain from making such orders (see eg the discussion of 'special reasons' in *Chapter 7*)
- contributing to discussion in court if there are doubts about whether or not the court has certain powers—but without seeking to influence the sentencing decision
- making specific applications, eg for the forfeiture of property, weapons, or drugs (*Chapter 5*)
- reminding the court of relevant ancillary powers (*Chapter 5*).

There is provision, once the relevant part of the Crime (Sentences) Act 1997 is in force, for certain prosecutors to be shown pre-sentence reports (PSRs) and to comment upon these. Such comment will presumably be to challenge aspects of a PSR which do not accord with prosecutor's view of events, or to comment from the victim's perspective: see *Chapter 4* concerning victims generally.

Once the basic facts of the offence are established a further information gathering process begins—which may involve questions from the bench. The aim is for the court to have before it as much relevant information as is appropriate to the case. The extent of this information will depend on the nature of the case. Generally, the more serious the offence and the more severe the likely outcome, the greater the need to explore additional items. The information might include:

Previous convictions

The prosecutor will provide a list of any previous convictions (courts should be alert to the fact that recent convictions may not appear on such lists). Defence advocates may have difficulty if they know that the list is incomplete. Whereas they are officers of the court, they also owe a duty to their client which would prevent their disclosing omissions without express consent. When defence solicitors are asked to confirm the list they may properly invite the court to put that question directly to the offender.

The list should be in chronological order and will often be submitted for speed and convenience by way of a computer printout. Under the Rehabilitation of Offenders Act 1974 certain convictions can become 'spent' by effluxion of time, ie the offender may (subject to exceptions) lawfully deny their existence when asked about them. The time within which convictions become 'spent' depends on factors such as the type and length of sentence imposed and the offender's age at the time. Conviction of a further offence during what is known as the 'rehabilitation period' can extend the original period to the expiry of the later period. The operation of the 1974 Act is, therefore, somewhat complex and lists of previous convictions may not always accurately reflect which offences are truly 'spent'. However, when sentencing, courts are, in any event, specifically entitled to receive details of *all* previous convictions, including any which are spent (but which should still be marked as such) and to accord them such relevance as appears appropriate. 📖🖐

The potential effect of previous convictions and responses to sentences imposed for them is discussed in *Chapter 6*.

Antecedents

The list of previous convictions is sometimes called the defendant's 'antecedents'. Strictly speaking, antecedents are wider, including eg details about family, employment, regular financial commitments and so on. Such details may be provided, if known, subject to local practice.

Cautions

The practice of issuing a caution (ie a formal warning) to offenders rather than prosecuting them is non-statutory and operates at the discretion of the chief constable of an area. Home Office circulars have sought to produce consistency. Normally, the decision to caution will have been made before a prosecution is launched, but the High Court has indicated that the Crown prosecutor must, when reviewing a case, consider whether a caution is preferable to continuing with the prosecution. In trying to set informal national standards for cautioning, the Home Office has advised that cautions should be cited to the court at the sentencing stage by the prosecutor only where relevant to the offence under consideration and by way of a list separate from the previous convictions (see generally Home Office Circulars 59/1990; 18/1994). It is for courts to decide what relevance to attach to a caution. The offence will have been admitted, but without those protections afforded by a court of law. It will have been accepted as an alternative to prosecution. But a caution will indicate that an offender has been warned about previous behaviour, possibly of a similar kind, and this may serve to cancel out mitigation which relies on ignorance.

Driving licences and DVLA printouts

It is essential for a court to see either the driving licence or a DVLA printout where a road traffic offence is endorsable or attracts disqualification from driving: *Chapter 7*.

TICs

The practice of defendants asking for outstanding offences—for which they have *not* been prosecuted—to be taken into consideration (known as 'TICs') is a non-statutory means of encouraging offenders to make a clean breast of matters. It disposes of possible further cases easily and quickly. The sentence should reflect any TICs and the court should make an appropriate announcement and keep a record of the relevant offences. The maximum sentence remains that for the offence *charged* (or the maximum aggregate sentence where applicable: *Chapter 3*).

An application should normally only be allowed where the substantive offences and the TICs are either way offences (see *Chapter 1*) and of a similar nature. Endorsable offences should not generally be allowed as TICs, since the offender might escape 'totting-up' or a mandatory disqualification (*Chapter 7*). Usually, the prosecutor prepares a written list of the TICs for adoption by the defendant at the hearing. If he or she decides not to accept the list, or rejects part of it, the court must disregard the list or relevant part. The prosecutor then has to decide whether or not to bring formal charges instead.

Mitigation

The defendant will often put forward information to support a request for leniency—usually called 'mitigation'. A poor record reduces the scope for mitigation. Mitigation may relate:

- to the *offence* (when it should be considered along with other seriousness factors in arriving at the correct sentence level); or
- to the *offender*—often called 'personal mitigation' or 'offender mitigation', which can reduce a sentence below that which the seriousness of the offence would itself merit. Personal mitigation might include, eg a character reference, a supportive letter from an employer, details of unusually difficult financial circumstances, ill-health or domestic difficulties.

The court must consider each case on its merits and decide what factors are relevant—as well as the extent to which these ought to be taken into account. It should be clear in the court's mind which kind of mitigation is under consideration, and its effect, if any, on the decision.

A legal representative mitigates 'on instructions' from his or her client and will not usually know whether the information supplied by the client is correct. He or she cannot (and should not be expected to) guarantee its validity—but must never knowingly mislead the court. Courts can call for verification if necessary (eg by direct proof or by investigation within a PSR, if appropriate).

Derogatory assertions

Sometimes in seeking to offer mitigation the defendant will make assertions which impugn the character of other people, including possibly that of the victim. The court will naturally wish to balance the defendant's right to mitigate with the interests of other people (who, more often than not, will not be present in court). Section 58 Criminal Procedure and Investigations Act 1996 provides that if there are substantial grounds for believing that an assertion is:

- derogatory of another; *and*
- false or irrelevant to sentence

the court may make certain restrictions on the public reporting of the assertion. Obviously, once a court considers *any* mitigation to be irrelevant it should prohibit that line of mitigation being pursued. However, the right of a defendant to mitigate must never be improperly constrained. Advice should be taken: 📖🖐

Written pleas of guilty—Section 12 Magistrates' Courts Act 1980

Where the prosecutor has adopted the written plea procedure in relation to a summary offence (usually known as 'MCA', 'section 12' or the 'guilty by post' procedure) all the information will be contained in the statutory documents: a prosecution 'statement of facts'; the defendant's written plea and any written mitigation; and occasionally a notice to cite previous convictions. The offender may address the court in person if he or she attends. Mitigation can concern the offence or the offender's personal circumstances.

Financial circumstances

Where a financial penalty or compensation is in mind, the court can order the defendant to provide a statement of his or her 'financial circumstances'. The statement can be provided in writing or be given orally in court. There are criminal penalties for failure to provide the statement, or for giving false information: see *Chapter 3*.

Pre-sentence reports

The court may require a probation officer or social worker to complete a written pre-sentence report (PSR) to assist the court '. . . in determining the most suitable method' of dealing with the offender. This will require an adjournment, usually for three weeks but often for a shorter period if the offender is already known to the Probation Service and/or is to be remanded in custody. In certain instances, the court is obliged to obtain a PSR—unless it considers this unnecessary. PSRs are considered in *Chapter 8*.

Medical reports

The court can order a report about the offender's physical or mental condition. Psychiatric reports are discussed in *Chapter 10*.

DEFERMENT OF SENTENCE

Deferment is designed to deal with the situation where—because of what a court has discovered about the offender—it considers that it is right to postpone the sentencing decision in order to 'have regard . . . to his conduct after conviction or to any change in his circumstances'. The defendant must consent to the deferment. The maximum period for which sentence can be deferred is six months. There is no power to remand an offender or make him or her subject to any requirements or restrictions during this period and the court, in deferring sentence, cannot make ancillary orders except for an interim driving disqualification or a restitution order. It should be noted that:

- deferment may only be used *once* in respect of any offence. There are no restrictions as to the offence

- the court must ensure that the offender understands exactly what is being proposed and to what he or she is being asked to consent. (The general principle is that offenders have a right to know their fate as soon as possible after conviction)
- the interests of the victim must be considered. Postponing sentence may mean postponing formal compensation.

The offender must consent to the deferment, and the court must be satisfied, having regard to the nature of the offence and the character and circumstances of the offender, that it would be in the interest of justice to defer sentence. The Court of Appeal has given guidance:

> The consent of the defendant must be obtained . . . the court should make it clear . . . what the particular purposes are which the court has in mind and what conduct is expected of [the offender] during the deferment. The deferring court should make a careful note of the purposes for which the sentence is being deferred and what steps, if any, it expects the accused to take during the period of deferment.

A specific object should be in mind. Deferment should *not* be used to avoid the sentencing decision. Again, the Court of Appeal has said that:

> The purpose of deferment is to enable the court to take into account the defendant's conduct after conviction or any change in circumstances and then only if it is in the interest of justice to exercise the power . . . the power is not to be used as an easy way out for a court which is unable to make up its mind.

Also, deferment should not be used simply to secure a result which could be achieved by a requirement in a probation order, eg continuing with a course of medical treatment; and care must be taken not to allow an offender to 'buy' his or her way out of a prison sentence.

Reasons

Reasons should be given to the offender and recorded by the court about the purposes of the deferment—so that he or she is fully aware of what is expected during the deferment period. The court should also indicate how it wishes to be informed about whether the offender has met its expectations—ie usually by way of an updated PSR.

End of the deferment period

It is desirable (but not legally essential) that the magistrates who ordered the deferment should sit to impose sentence. The later bench should consider the reasons for the deferment and the nature of any expectations placed on the offender, and determine whether the offender has substantially adhered to what was expected. If he or she has done so, then a custodial sentence ought not generally to be imposed. If the defendant has not complied with the terms of the deferment, the court should state in what regard.

Further offence committed during the period of deferment
If the offender commits another offence during the deferment, the court which convicts him of that offence may deal with the deferred case even though the period has not expired. If the court which deferred sentence was the Crown Court, then the offender should be committed back to that court to be dealt with.

COMMITTAL FOR SENTENCE

A magistrates' court can commit an offender to the Crown Court to be sentenced in a variety of situations. The most common of these is where he or she is convicted of an either way offence (formally or pursuant to the section 49 plea before venue procedure: see above) and the court is of the opinion that the offence is so serious that greater punishment should be inflicted than magistrates can impose. In the case of a sexual or violent offence (page 60) there is an alternative basis for committal, ie that a sentence of imprisonment for a term longer than the magistrates have power to impose is necessary to protect the public from serious harm from the offender. Accordingly, if magistrates are dealing with *one* either way offence, they will need to be of opinion that the offence merits a custodial sentence of more than six months before committing for sentence. If dealing with two or more offences, they would be contemplating consecutive custodial sentences totalling longer than 12 months: see *Chapter 3*. Case law suggests that consecutive sentences usually arise only where eg:

- offences are of a totally different nature from each other; or
- have been committed on totally separate occasions; or
- have been committed on bail.

In practice, committal is usually likely to occur only where magistrates believe that the sentence which the Crown Court would pass is likely to be significantly higher than one that they themselves would pass: see *Appendix B* to this handbook.

Following a section 49 indication of a guilty plea (above) the court must look at all relevant factors and will commit for sentence if, in the final analysis, it feels that its powers are inadequate. Where the 'mode of trial' procedure for an either way offence has been followed, the same factors and powers will need to be considered on the defendant pleading guilty or being found guilty by the magistrates.

The main considerations are likely to be the seriousness of the offence or offences, previous convictions and whether any custodial sentences should be concurrent or consecutive. The effect of credit for a guilty plea is always highly relevant in borderline cases. 📖✋

The council of the Justices' Clerks' Society has advised its members that:

> . . . greatest credit should be given where a guilty plea is entered before the magistrates' court. Credit will continue to be given where a guilty plea is entered for the first time in the Crown Court but that credit will normally be less than where the plea was entered in the magistrates' court where there is power to do so. (*JCS News Sheet* No. 97/63: December 1997)

Mode of trial decisions (page 25) whether summary trial or trial at the Crown Court is more appropriate involve the magistrates' court in considering the main seriousness factors *prior* to accepting jurisdiction. Good practice suggests that if magistrates do assume jurisdiction to deal with an either way case they should normally only use their power to commit the offender to the Crown Court for sentence where new factors emerge—such as previous convictions (which are only presented *after* a defendant is convicted). But care should be taken that these do in fact affect the seriousness of the offence: *Chapter 6*. Other new information may emerge from the evidence in the case or because the full facts create a different impression to the original outline of the case by the prosecutor. However, the High Court has confirmed that a magistrates' court may commit for sentence if, on reconsidering the appropriateness of its original decision as to venue in the light of all the facts which have subsequently emerged, the seriousness of the offence warrants a sentence in excess of magistrates' own powers.

An offender who is committed for sentence may also be committed to be dealt with by the Crown Court for certain other offences even though the magistrates' sentencing powers for these extra offences would otherwise have been sufficient. 📖✋

Magistrates also have powers to commit for sentence in certain other situations 📖✋:

- someone who is an absconder and who should have appeared in that court
- on breach of an order or sentence of the Crown Court, eg a community service order; or
- where the offender committed the offence during a Crown Court suspended sentence of imprisonment.

Other circumstances include where a prisoner subject to early release (*Chapter 9*) commits an imprisonable offence during the original period of a custodial sentence and is liable to be returned to prison to serve more than six months.

Once an offender has been committed for sentence, any ancillary orders should be left to the Crown Court—apart, possibly, from an interim driving disqualification (see *Chapter 7*).

Bail or custody on committal to the Crown Court for sentence?

The conventional wisdom was that it would be incongruous for a court to conclude that a defendant deserves a longer sentence and then to release him or her on bail. The following advice from the council of the Justices' Clerks' Society to members has been endorsed by the Lord Chief Justice (*JCS News Sheet* No. 97/63: December 1997):

> There are differing views on whether or not a defendant committed for sentence should normally be committed in custody. The two main lines of argument are that:
>
> 1. A committal for sentence presupposes a decision by the magistrates that a defendant would receive a substantial custodial sentence and therefore committal should be in custody.
> 2. The defendant's status after committal should normally be the same as that before committal, that is a defendant on bail up to committal will normally remain on bail after committal and a defendant in custody will normally remain in custody.
>
> It is the view of the council of the Society that the determining criterion should be the defendant's status before committal. Council considers that the authorities usually relied upon are largely based on the need to prevent a defendant going in and out of custody throughout the course of the proceedings and that there is no need for a defendant on bail up to committal to be committed in custody unless the court has substantial grounds for believing that the defendant will fail to surrender to the court or will commit further offences.
>
> Council advises that courts should proceed on this basis. This advice is endorsed by the Lord Chief Justice.

The general right to bail in the Bail Act 1976 does not extend to a committal for sentence.

The Sentencing Framework

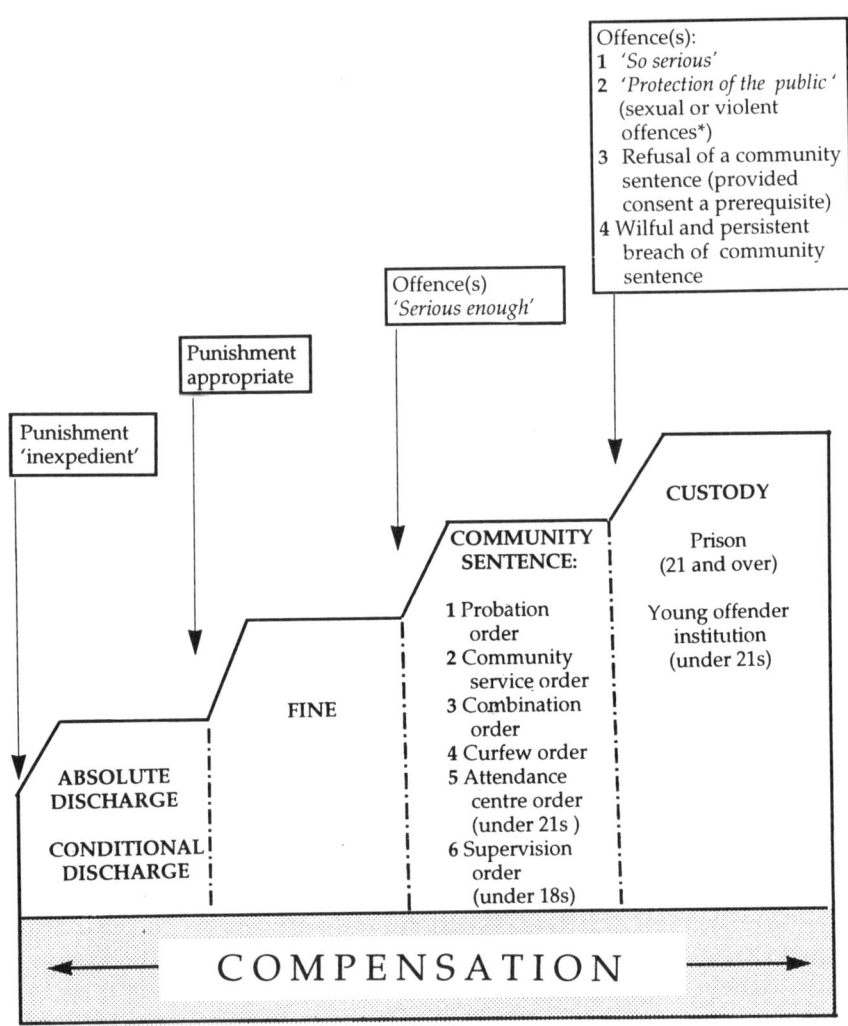

Figure 1

*All references in this handbook to sexual or violent offences are to these offences as defined in the Criminal Justice Act 1991: see page 60.

Chapter 3

The Four Levels of Sentence

As indicated in *Chapter 2*, good practice indicates that sentencers should adopt a structured approach to decision-making. This chapter contains:

- a diagram of the *Sentencing Framework* (*Figure 1* on page 38)
- an explanation of the main elements of each sentencing option
- an example of a decision-making structure: *A Structured Guide to Sentencing* (*Figure 2* on pages 66 and 67).

THE SENTENCING FRAMEWORK

Figure 1 contains an outline of the sentencing framework which resulted from the Criminal Justice Act 1991 (as amended). It should be noted that each level of sentence is affected by statutory 'threshold' criteria:

- **DISCHARGES**: punishment is 'inexpedient'.
- **FINES**: by implication punishment *is* expedient (but more severe punishment is inappropriate). The size of a fine must reflect the seriousness of the offence *and* the offender's financial circumstances.
- **COMMUNITY SENTENCES**: the offence is 'serious enough'. The degree of 'restriction of liberty' must be commensurate with the seriousness of the offence *and* the particular order(s) suitable for the offender
- **CUSTODY**:
  — the offence is so serious that *only* such a sentence can be justified; or
  — if the offence is a sexual or violent offence (see page 60), 'only such a sentence would be adequate to protect the public from serious harm' from the offender; or
  — the offender has refused to consent to one of the few types of community sentence still requiring such consent (see page 50). Custody is also possible on breach of some community sentences following 'wilful and persistent' failure to comply.

The length of a custodial sentence must be commensurate with the seriousness of the offence or, as appropriate, the need to protect the public from serious harm from a sexual or violent offender.

In most cases, the seriousness of the offence determines which of the four levels of sentence should be considered and the extent of any penalty within that level. Any number of associated offences can be taken into account when assessing seriousness: *Chapter 1*.

DISCHARGES

> CRITERION: '. . . having regard to the circumstances including the nature of the offence and the character of the offender . . . it is inexpedient to inflict punishment . . .'

> RESTRICTION ON LIBERTY: none implied or arising.

Absolute discharge
This marks the conviction but no other obligations follow. An absolute discharge may be appropriate when the offence is of a truly minor nature, purely technical, or when there are several offences and a comparatively trivial one requires a residual sentencing disposal (which might equally be achieved by imposing 'no separate penalty': below).

Conditional discharge
This makes the offender subject to a single condition, ie that no further offence is committed within a period of up to three years—as set by the court. Conviction of *any* criminal offence during this 'operational period' renders the offender liable to be re-sentenced for the offence which originally gave rise to the discharge—in addition to any sentence for the new offence. There is no monitoring of the offender's behaviour or supervision during the period of the discharge.

The court must explain the effects of the order to the offender. For this reason it is often argued that a conditional discharge cannot be imposed in the offender's absence, and not on a company.

Some people argue that a conditional discharge can be used at any level of seriousness, even instead of imprisonment on occasion, eg to give an offender a fresh start. This depends on how courts interpret the phrase 'punishment is inexpedient' and whether this approach can be reconciled with the fact that, in the example given, the custody threshold will have been reached (though it is clearly established that personal mitigation relating to the offender can justify a less severe sentence when the seriousness of the offence might have justified a more severe one). Magistrates should check what view is taken locally and seek advice if faced with these or similar arguments. 📖⌖

Breach of conditional discharge

A 'breach' occurs if a fresh criminal offence is *committed* during the operational period. When the court comes to re-sentence the offender for the original offence, the seriousness of that offence has to be considered anew. Apart from substituting a different disposal, the court has the option of taking no action and allowing the conditional discharge to run if it thinks this is the proper course.

Breach of a conditional discharge imposed by a magistrates' court can be dealt with anywhere in England and Wales (subject to the consent of the original court if in a different place). Magistrates cannot deal with a Crown Court conditional discharge (but must inform that court of the breach) unless imposed on appeal from a magistrates' court.

FINES

> **CRITERION**: this is not directly covered by statute. By implication, fines should be used where a discharge is not appropriate, ie where punishment *is* expedient—but a more severe sentence would not be. The *size* of a fine must reflect the seriousness of the offence *and* the offender's financial circumstances.

> **RESTRICTION ON LIBERTY**: fines do not affect the physical liberty of the offender, but a loss of spending power deprives the offender of the ability to direct money towards recreation and leisure, or to choose how he or she spends a sum of money equivalent to the amount of the fine.

In magistrates' courts the maximum fine is set by statute, in most instances by reference to one of five standard levels. Values are updated by Parliament from time to time. At the time of writing they are:

Level 1	£200
Level 2	£500
Level 3	£1,000
Level 4	£2,500
Level 5	£5,000

Fines for individual either way offences tried summarily are usually restricted to a maximum figure of £5,000. If no maximum is specified (which is rare) then Level 3 applies. There is no over-arching, aggregate limit affecting multiple offences (as eg there is with imprisonment). The global ceiling is, in effect, determined by the proportionality principle and by the offender's own financial circumstances: below. Maximum fines in the Crown Court are often not subject to any legal limit.

Fixing the amount of the fine

This involves the court in the following tasks:

- reflecting the seriousness of the offence
- an inquiry into the 'financial circumstances' of the offender
- taking these into account (so far as they are known or appear)
- taking all other circumstances into account.

Financial circumstances

Courts can increase or decrease the size of a fine according to an individual offender's financial circumstances. Where there are several fines (and/or compensation or costs) the court must bear in mind the total impact on the offender's finances and may need to make downwards adjustments and/or extend the time for payment.

The term 'financial circumstances' appears to be wide in scope. It probably covers not only direct income but also eg savings, investments, endowment policies and valuable possessions, as well as permitting a court to consider the position of, say, an offender with no apparent income but who is living a fairly lavish lifestyle, based possibly on a partner's support—which thereby reduces the need for personal expenditure. This last point is yet to be tested on appeal in the higher courts. The former law (which was based on the concept of 'means') was against eg family income being taken into account.

Financial penalties should usually be set at a level which envisages payment within a maximum of 12 months (but possibly up to two or even three years in appropriate cases, usually where compensation is concerned).

In the case of people on state benefits (especially income support which is essentially set at subsistence level) the amount of each instalment may well have to be kept to the minimum and the number of instalments reduced to enable payment over a matter of months if not weeks. This principle will obviously apply equally to other people with very limited income. Thus in the important case of *R v Stockport Justices, ex parte Conlon* (*The Times*, 3 January 1997), Lord Justice Staughton expressed concerns about the amount of fines in respect of defendants with limited means, stating:

> What troubles me about these cases is not the remedies which the magistrates had to choose from as means of enforcement, but the size of the fines which those on income support were expected to pay out of resources that are said to be only sufficient for the necessities of life. I can see that

over a short period of time the money provided as income support may be sufficient for paying a small but regular amount towards fines but as everybody knows there are contingencies which occur and will strain a tight budget to breaking point. That, I think is what the probation officer had in mind when he spoke of regularly fining £10 a fortnight over a period of 52 weeks. The fact that, in an ordinary week, there will be £5 available does not by any means lead to the conclusion that there will be no difficulty in every week of the year. I would prefer a solution where fines on those of limited means were lesser in amount—or at least lesser in total—so that they could be paid in a matter of weeks, and where regular payment was firmly enforced. But that is another story from what we are required to decide today.

Financial circumstances orders

After conviction, defendants can be made subject to a 'financial circumstances order' (or *before* conviction if they have written pleading guilty under the written plea of guilty procedure: *Chapter 2*). The defendant is then required to provide such a statement of his or her financial circumstances as the court may require. This may be by way of written details or in answer to inquiries in court. Failure to comply is an offence punishable by a Level 3 fine (£1,000). False or incomplete disclosure is a separate offence carrying three months imprisonment and/or a Level 4 fine (£2,500).

Combining fines with other sentences

Fines are capable of being imposed in addition to custody for a single offence. The general view appears to be either that a fine *and* a community sentence cannot be imposed for a single offence, or that this would be inappropriate even if technically permissible. 📖✋ The possibility of a fine and a discharge for a single offence can hardly arise given the criterion for discharges (ie 'punishment is inexpedient', above). Ancillary orders can always be added to a fine: *Chapters 5 and 7.*

A compensation order can be made on its own or combined with any other sentence. However, if *both* a fine and compensation are considered appropriate and the offender cannot realistically be ordered to pay both in full because of his or her financial circumstances then the compensation order *must* always be preferred at the expense of the fine (and by implication any prosecution costs): see further *Chapter 4.*

Excise penalties

Certain convictions result in the imposition of an excise penalty rather than a fine. The most common example is the offence of using or keeping an untaxed motor vehicle, although there are many Customs and Excise offences leading to similar penalties. In these cases:

- the full amount of the penalty is payable unless mitigated by the court
- any excise penalties collected by the court will be paid over direct to the Commissioners of Customs and Excise unless the Commissioners direct otherwise (as they have done eg in respect of untaxed motor vehicles where penalties are paid over to the Lord Chancellor along with ordinary fines)
- excise penalties cannot be remitted in enforcement proceedings on account of a 'subsequent change in circumstances': see below.

Otherwise, generally speaking, such penalties are collected and enforced in the same way as fines.

Payment and collection of fines
Fines, compensation and costs are due and payable forthwith unless the court orders otherwise—and offenders cannot automatically expect 'easy terms'. As appropriate, payment can be allowed by a fixed date or by instalments. Payment can be made in various ways including:

- cash (within the normal limits of legal tender, ie large amounts of small currency need not be accepted)
- postal order
- cheque (with or without a guarantee card. The court can refuse to accept a cheque especially if it has doubts as to whether it will be honoured)
- bank giro credit (standing order or *ad hoc* payments) if the court operates such a system
- credit card (if the court has adopted or is experimenting with this method).

Payments received by the court are applied in the following order:

- compensation
- costs
- fine.

If the offender is already subject to a suspended committal order for non-payment of an earlier account (see below), that account will, in practice, be credited first unless the offender requests otherwise.

Remission and alteration of fines
A later court has power to remit a fine, in whole or in part, in the light of any subsequent change in circumstances. This will often be in enforcement proceedings. A separate power allows a later court to remit all or part of a fine where it was originally fixed in the offender's

absence or without an adequate statement of financial circumstances if information before the later court suggests that, had the original court had that information, it would have fixed a lower fine or no fine at all. However, it is not possible to substitute a different type of penalty if such new information suggests that a fine was not appropriate in the first place. A compensation order cannot be remitted in the way that a fine can, but it can be discharged or reduced by a later court in limited circumstances: see *Chapter 4*. If necessary, seek advice. 📖 ✋

Immediate enforcement
The following measures are applicable to all types of financial order:

Power to search
On imposing the fine (or eg in enforcement proceedings) magistrates can order the offender to be searched—usually by a police officer or gaoler—and that any monies found belonging to the offender be applied to meeting sums due. Regard must be had to domestic needs.

Immediate custody 📖 ✋
There are three circumstances in which magistrates can order custody in default (immediate or suspended as appropriate) at the time of imposing a fine:

- where the offence is imprisonable and the offender appears to have the means to pay forthwith (which might include withdrawing money from a savings account)
- where it appears that the offender is unlikely to remain long enough at a place of abode in the UK to allow enforcement of the fine by other means (eg a person of no fixed abode or who is about to go abroad indefinitely)
- the offender is on the same occasion *sentenced* to immediate custody or is already serving such a *sentence* (ie not as a result of *committal* for some other default).

General enforcement powers
In all other circumstances the full enforcement process applies and a subsequent enquiry must be held into the default. It is often said that good enforcement begins at the point of imposition. If the size of a fine is assessed carefully and an appropriate order made for payment, then there should be a greater chance of compliance and a sound baseline from which to address any default. On imposing financial penalties courts can set a review hearing date when enforcement will be considered if payment has not been made. Alternatively, computerised accounts programmes can respond immediately by way of a:

45

- reminder
- summons
- warrant backed for bail
- warrant without bail
- distress warrant.

Once the enforcement process is in being (and subject in most cases to the defaulter being before the court) there are various options:

- to set further terms for payment
- search (as described above)
- an attachment of earnings order (ie to an employer)
- a request to deduct the fine from income support
- a distress warrant to seize the offender's goods (either immediately or suspended on terms)
- an attendance centre order which, since 1 October 1997, is available for defaulters aged up to 24 years inclusive
- a money payment supervision order (usually operated by the probation service or a court's own 'civilian enforcement officer')
- detention in the court precincts or at a police station until 8 pm
- overnight detention in a police station
- imprisonment, or detention if the offender is below 21 years of age, within a scale which relates maximum periods to amounts outstanding. Either type of order can be suspended on terms
- application to the High Court or county court for civil remedies
- remission (above).

Additionally, curfews/electronic monitoring, community service and disqualification from driving for fine default are being tested in certain areas. Seek advice locally: 📖✋.

Where magistrates are considering detention of an offender below 21 years of age, they must be satisfied that it is undesirable or impractical to make a money payment supervision order and this must be stated in the warrant. Additionally the court must:

- with regard to all age ranges consider or try all options other than custody; and
- where the defaulter is under 21 years, be satisfied that no other method is appropriate; when it must state in open court the reason for this opinion and cause the reason to be specified in the warrant of commitment and to be entered in the court register.

This handbook does not deal further with these powers which are fraught with technical difficulties. Advice should be taken, especially where custody is in prospect. 📖✋

COMMUNITY SENTENCES

THRESHOLD CRITERION: '. . . the offence, or the combination of the offence and one or more offences associated with it, [is] serious enough to warrant such a sentence.' This criterion applies to *all* six community orders below, ie the community sentence threshold must be reached *before* a particular order or orders can be chosen.

RESTRICTION ON LIBERTY: all community sentences place demands on the offender's time, energies or activities. The extent of the restriction must be ' . . . commensurate with the seriousness of the offence, or the combination of the offence and one or more offences associated with it.'

SUITABILITY: There is an extra (and sometimes conflicting consideration) in that the community order or orders selected must be the most suitable for the offender: see below.

Associated offences

The meaning of associated offences is outlined in *Chapter 1*.

The six community orders

A community sentence is '. . . a sentence which consists of or includes one or more community orders'. This enables courts to tailor individual decisions by selecting one or more orders from the menu of six community orders, even theoretically for a single offence: but see further under the heading *Combining community sentences, page 49*. The six community orders are:

- probation order (with or without added requirements)
- community service order
- combination order
- attendance centre order: under 21 years of age only (contrast the age limit for fine defaulters, ie up to 24 inclusive: page 46)
- curfew order
- supervision order (under 18 years of age only).

Restriction on liberty and suitability

Once the court is satisfied that the offence or offences are 'serious enough' to warrant a community sentence, two main considerations arise:

47

- the community order (or orders) must be the 'most suitable for the offender'
- the restriction on liberty arising from the community order (or orders) must be commensurate with the seriousness of the offence or offences.

The sentencer thus has a dual responsibility: that of deciding on the appropriate degree of restriction on liberty (as determined by the seriousness of the offence or offences), whilst ensuring that the community order or orders is or are the most suitable for the offender. This balancing exercise is one which makes considerable demands on sentencer's skills, and requires close attention if fair, appropriate and consistent sentencing practices are to be maintained. The statutory provision which creates these considerations mentions suitability *before* restriction on liberty. This is the only clue as to how any conflict might be resolved, ie possibly in favour of suitability (except where a 'suitable' sentence would involve greater restriction of liberty than can be justified by the seriousness of the offence).

Core issues
Thus, sentencers need an understanding of certain core matters:

- the factors inherent in each type of offence which are likely to affect seriousness, whether as aggravating or mitigating factors
- any personal and other factors which may be relevant to seriousness (eg previous convictions: *Chapter 6,* or in some instances the offender's circumstances: see pages 22, 31)
- what value to place on each of these factors so as to ensure a fair and consistent approach—taking account of good sentencing practice and local guidelines
- what each type of community order seeks to achieve and what demands it makes on an offender
- the comparative restriction on liberty which each of the six community orders places on the offender's liberty—and how these restrictions correlate in terms of duration, intensity, frequency and effect on offenders.

Liaison with the probation service
There is a need for a dialogue between sentencers and probation officers who write PSRs and supervise community orders—and hopefully an understanding on key matters. Many local probation areas and courts have entered into such dialogue, often through Probation Liaison Committees, on three broad fronts by:

- providing courts with detailed information about the nature and level of contact with offenders subject to community orders and discussing practice requirements under Home Office/Probation Service *National Standards for the Supervision of Offenders in the Community*
- by agreeing a structure for common understanding about the relationship between levels of seriousness and the restrictions on liberty which arise from the various community orders (sometimes called a 'sentencing grid' or 'matrix')
- local 'protocols' and statements of preferred practice (page 104) covering various aspects of Probation Service responsibilities.

Factors relevant to assessing seriousness
A note of some general factors affecting the assessment of seriousness is contained in *Chapter 2* under the heading *Structured Decision-making*.

Some factors relevant to 'suitability'
Bearing in mind the offender based factors already outlined in relation to the seriousness of the offence in *Chapter 2*, the following may be particularly relevant to the *suitability* of an order or orders for an individual offender.

— the type of restriction on liberty and effort or input required
— family or work commitments
— health issues
— the age of the offender
— the offender's mobility or lack of mobility
— the perceived cause of offending
— the offender's own needs to enable him or her to turn away from offending
— the offender's general ability and motivation to undertake and complete the order
— the offender's consent to or his or her willingness to comply with the order (where relevant: see page 50) or his or her motivation
— any risk of re-offending
— the protection of the public
— the prevention of future offending by the offender
— any responses to previous sentences by the offender and especially to community orders.

Combining community orders
A community sentence may contain (subject to one limitation and any age restrictions) one or more of the six community orders. The

49

limitation is that probation and community service can only be combined by way of a combination order. The extent to which the facility to combine orders might be exercised seems not to have troubled courts who appear, on the whole, to have adhered to the previous practice whereby there could be only one distinct disposal for each offence. In constructing a community sentence containing multiple orders the court must consider the overall restriction of liberty and be careful not to arrive at a *disproportionate* sentence. Advice may be desirable. 📖✍

Despite the apparent intention of Parliament at the time of the Criminal Justice Act 1991, some opinion appears to be against using both a fine and community sentence for a single offence—although this is a possibility in relation to separate offences.

By statute, a probation order cannot be made at the same time as a suspended sentence of imprisonment, even in respect of a separate offence: Powers of Criminal Courts Act 1973.

Ancillary orders such as compensation, costs, endorsement and disqualification can always be added to a community sentence. Compensation must be considered in appropriate cases: see *Chapter 4.*

Pre-sentence reports

In considering the question of suitability, the court must take into account any information before it about the offender. The court must normally obtain and consider a pre-sentence report (PSR) before deciding on the suitability for the offender of:

- a probation order with added requirements
- a community service order
- a combination order
- a supervision order with special requirements (under 18s only).

Failure to comply with this requirement will not, of itself, render the sentence invalid and, indeed, the court can deem a PSR to be 'unnecessary'. Good practice, nevertheless suggests that a PSR should normally be called for in circumstances where any form of community order is being considered: see generally *Chapter 8.*

Consents and explanations

On 1 October 1997, under the Crime (Sentences) Act 1997, the need for offenders to consent to, or express a willingness to comply with, community orders was largely dispensed with. Such 'agreement' is now *only* required in relation to probation orders with additional requirements relating to treatment for a mental condition or drug/alcohol dependency (page 53). (The situations in which custody can be imposed because of unwillingness to undertake a community order are thus correspondingly fewer). In other situations offenders who might at first indicate that they are not willing to undertake, say, community service can now be made subject to a community service order nonetheless.

Magistrates need to proceed with caution if considering an order when they know the offender lacks motivation, but equally he or she cannot be seen to be dictating to the court. The probation service will face extra pressures if it has unwilling people to contend with. However, 'wilful and persistent' breach of any community order (whether or not consent remains necessary at the outset) still appears to permit custody as an option on revocation provided the original offence carried imprisonment: see *Breach of Community Orders*, page 58.

In those few situations where consent *is* still required (above), a refusal allows the imposition of custody at the outset, again assuming that the offence carries imprisonment. This is so even if the particular offence was not deemed so serious in the first place. Similarly, custody can be used on breach of the order: page 58.

The fact that refusal to consent to some community orders can lead to a custodial sentence need not preclude the court from considering other forms of community (or financial) order to which the offender might consent, or for which consent is not required. Again, care must be taken that the offender is not dictating his or her own terms.

There is in respect of most community orders an obligation to explain to the offender the effect of the proposed order. This is good practice in any event—and a precursor to obtaining full and informed consent or an expression of willingness to comply where required.

PROBATION

The probation order is a sentence in its own right—not, as was once the case, an order in lieu of sentence. The order can be made whether or not the maximum sentence for an offence includes imprisonment. The statutory purposes of probation are:

- to secure the offender's rehabilitation; or
- to protect the public from harm from the offender; or
- to prevent further offences by the offender.

Effect of a probation order

The offender is placed under the supervision of a probation officer for the area in which he or she resides or will reside. The offender must keep in touch with the supervising officer in accordance with instructions which the latter may give, and notify the officer of any change of address. These are sometimes called 'standard requirements'.

Duration

A probation order lasts for such period as the court decides—not less than six months nor more than three years.

Pre-sentence reports

Only probation orders containing additional requirements must by law be preceded by a PSR (unless the court deems a PSR unnecessary). Seemingly, most courts accept that it is usually undesirable to make even a basic probation order without full information.

Willingness to comply 📖🖐

Since 1 October 1997 *only* probation orders with requirements relating to treatment for mental condition or drug/alcohol dependency require an expression of willingness to comply on the part of the offender.

Additional requirements 📖🖐

If felt desirable for any of the statutory purposes of probation (above) the court may insert one or more additional requirements ie:

- *a requirement as to residence.* This could be:
  —residence in an approved probation hostel managed by the probation service or a voluntary organization.
  —at a non approved hostel or other institution such as a dependency clinic which may tackle drug or alcohol addictions (some of which are private organizations).
  —a requirement to reside where directed by the probation officer. This is likely to be in the offender's home area at a private address considered suitable by the probation officer and will restrict the offender from moving without first seeking approval from the probation officer.
- *a requirement to attend (i) a probation centre or (ii) other specified activities for up to 60 days*
  —a probation centre is a resource approved by the Secretary of State offering an intensive programme which addresses offending behaviour and its various causes. Offenders are expected to attend for a full day and for as many days as is necessary (up to 60 days in all) to complete the programme. Probation centres are usually for those at the top end of the 'serious enough' scale.
  —specified activities are approved locally by the probation committee. Offenders can be required to attend a specified activity—eg an alcohol education group—for up to 60 days or a range of activities according to their needs (eg an offending behaviour group, an anger management course, a substance

misuse group). A 'session' lasting for, say, two hours counts as a day.

—there is one exception to the 60 day maximum rule and this applies to sex offenders. There is no upper limit on the number of days for which attendance can be required (subject to this not exceeding the length of the probation order), but the court which imposes the requirement must specify the number of days the offender is required to attend a sex offenders' group (or other facility) when making the order.

- *a requirement to receive treatment for mental condition.* This condition can only be used when the court has an assessment from a psychiatrist and treatment is actually available from either a psychiatrist or chartered psychologist. Again, the requirement can be for the whole length of the probation order or for a part of this time as specified by the court.

- *a requirement to receive treatment for drug or alcohol dependency.* This refers to out-patient or residential facilities—usually for the seriously addicted. There is no restriction on the length of the requirement. It can be for the complete duration of the probation order or for a specific part of it, as determined by the court.

Other requirements

Courts have a general discretion to construct other requirements to meet special needs within the overall purposes of a probation order. This discretion should not be used to circumvent any of the statutory requirements. 📖✋

COMMUNITY SERVICE ORDERS

Under a community service order the offender is required to perform unpaid work in the community. A probation officer or someone employed by the probation service oversees the order. The offender must keep in touch with the relevant officer in accordance with instructions and notify him or her of any change of address. The offender must perform the hours of work as instructed, but instructions must, so far as practicable, not conflict with work, education or the offender's religious beliefs. The order has no inherent welfare content—and is mainly concerned with punishment and reparation.

Duration

The minimum number of hours is 40 and the maximum 240. The work must be performed within 12 months of the order being made, although the order remains in effect until the work is completed. It is possible to impose consecutive periods whether made on the same occasion or previously (advice is desirable 📖✋).

Imprisonable offences
A community service order can only be made if the maximum sentence for the offence includes imprisonment. However, orders are no longer seen as 'alternatives to custody' but as sentences in their own right.

Pre-sentence reports and 'assessment'
A PSR is required before imposing a community service order unless the court deems such a report to be unnecessary. There is, in any event, with community service a separate requirement whereby the court must be satisfied that the offender is a suitable person to perform work under such an order and that work is available—usually called a 'community service assessment' (which, unlike the PSR itself, can be oral or written). Care must be taken as to what is said when calling for a pre-sentence report: see *Chapter 8*.

Consent
Since 1 October 1997 the offender's consent is no longer required.

Extension of community service
In 1998 a limited number of courts will, in certain circumstances, be able to order a petty persistent offender to undergo community service instead of paying a fine even though the offence is non-imprisonable. Similarly, community service will be an experimental option in respect of fine default. 'Pilot courts' will receive details separately and magistrates in the relevant areas should seek advice locally. 📖✋

COMBINATION ORDERS

The combination order was created under the Criminal Justice Act 1991. It combines elements of the probation order and the community service order. This is the *only* way in which probation and community service can be imposed together for a single offence. There are no specific statutory purposes for combination orders, but the fact that the order incorporates elements of probation means that the purposes set out in relation to probation orders (above) are incorporated into the thinking behind that part of the order.

There is a single order even though the constituent parts are supervised or monitored separately. The offender is subject to the same obligations for each part of the order as he or she would be if each had been made independently. Thus eg restrictions concerning the effect of the community service part of the order on work, education and religion (page 53) equally apply.

Requirements can be added to the probation part of the order (see *Probation* above and where necessary seek advice: 📖✋). Attention must always be paid to the total restriction on liberty.

Duration
The combination order involves:

- a probation element of *at least* 12 months (as opposed to six months for 'straight probation') up to three years
- a community service element of between 40 and 100 hours (as compared to a maximum of 240 hours for a free-standing community service order).

Restriction of liberty and suitability
The nature of the combination order means that care needs to be taken when assessing the extent of restriction on liberty and the suitability of what may be a particularly demanding order for the offender in question—especially if requirements are to be added to the probation part of the order. The outcome must not be *disproportionate* to the offence.

Imprisonable offences
The maximum sentence for the offence must include imprisonment.

Pre-sentence reports
A PSR is required before imposing a combination order unless the court deems such a report to be unnecessary. There is, in any event, a separate requirement whereby the court must be satisfied in respect of the community service element that the offender is a suitable person to perform work under that part of the order and also that work is available—usually on the basis of a community service assessment. This aspect of an assessment/report may be oral or written.

Consent and willingness to comply
Since 1 October 1997 the offender needs to consent to a combination order only to the extent that there are requirements in the probation element which, if inserted in a free-standing probation order, would require consent: see under *Probation* above and page 50.

CURFEW ORDERS

The curfew order provisions are in force but only of practical effect in areas where courts have been notified that monitoring arrangements, electronic (see below) or otherwise, are available: check locally/📖✋.

Effect of a curfew order

The offender is required to remain, for periods specified in the order, at a particular place (usually, but not necessarily, his or her home) or places. Different places may be specified for different periods. The order is monitored by someone selected from a list of people specified for the purpose by the home secretary (and who may be drawn from the private sector). If the court so orders, monitoring may include electronic 'tagging' of the offender (see below).

Restrictions apply comparable to those for community service concerning the effect on work, education and religion: see page 53.

Duration

The order can be for between two and 12 hours a day which may be spread over one or more blocks. It can last for up to six months.

No need for an imprisonable offence

Curfew orders can be made in respect of *any* offence whether or not its maximum sentence includes imprisonment—although it should be remembered that the 'serious enough' test for a community sentence must be satisfied and the court must consider, in particular, the extent of the restriction of liberty imposed by the order.

Pre-sentence reports

There is no obligation to obtain a PSR. However, the court must obtain information about the place which it is proposed to specify in the order, and the effect that the order will have on people likely to be affected by the offender's presence at that place—pointing to the desirability of a PSR.

Willingness to comply

Since 1 October 1997 the offender's agreement is no longer required.

Trials of electronic monitoring

Trials of electronic monitoring in support of curfew orders first began in three areas of England and Wales in 1995 but are now more extensive.[1] In 1998 certain pilot courts will be able to make curfew orders combined

---

[1] For an overview see Dick Whitfield, *Tackling the Tag*, Waterside Press, 1997

with electronic monitoring in respect of non-payment of fines, persistent petty offenders (where further fines are not appropriate) and juvenile offenders. Magistrates in these areas will receive appropriate information.

ATTENDANCE CENTRE (UNDER 21s ONLY)

The purpose of an attendance centre order is that the offender be '. . . given, under supervision, appropriate occupation and instruction'. The order requires attendance at a specified centre and compliance with its rules. Centres are normally run by the police, sometimes with an input from other agencies. The regime is typically one of discipline, physical training, social awareness and social skills. A centre must be available within reasonable travelling distance for the offender: below.

Duration and prerequisites
Attendance centre orders are available for offenders aged ten to 20 years inclusive, although there are separate junior and senior facilities. In the case of adult offenders (ie those aged 18 to 20 inclusive) the order may be for between 12 and 36 hours. The court must fix the time of the first attendance but the centre organizer determines the length of attendances and further dates. There is a maximum attendance of three hours on any one day.

Pre-sentence reports
A PSR is not a prerequisite but special attention should be paid to the following:

- the centre must be reasonably accessible to the offender having regard to means of access, age and other relevant circumstances (centres for females, or 'mixed centres' are less common than those for males)
- as far as practicable, attendance must not interfere with school or work hours.

Imprisonable offences
The maximum sentence for the offence must include imprisonment.

Consent
The consent of the offender is not required and was not required even before the Crime (Sentences) Act 1997.

Fine default
Attendance centre orders can also used for fine defaulters up to age 24 inclusive: see page 46.

BREACH OF COMMUNITY ORDERS

Each community order is a self-contained disposal. Re-offending during the currency of an order does not, in itself, amount to a breach. Different provisions apply to failures to comply with the respective requirements of the different types of order.

Probation, community service, combination and curfew

Failure 'without reasonable excuse' to comply with a requirement of any of these orders can, on the matter being returned to court, result in one of the following outcomes:

- a fine of up to £1,000
- a community service order of up to 60 hours
- an attendance centre order (under 21s only)
- no action.

In each case the original community order continues to run. However, the court has the option to revoke the order and to re-sentence for the original offence. There is a requirement to give credit to the extent, if any, to which compliance occurred.

'Wilful and persistent' failure to comply with the terms of the order may, *if the original offence carried imprisonment,* result in a custodial sentence on revocation in the breach proceedings. In such a situation there is a legal (if fictional) assumption that the offender has refused to consent to a community order which required consent. This is a basis for a custodial sentence even if the seriousness of the original offence did not in itself warrant custody: see under *Custody,* below.

If the order was made by the Crown Court the breach, once established, must (except where the order was made on appeal against sentence from a magistrates' court) be referred back to the Crown Court if revocation and re-sentencing are to be considered.

Attendance centre orders

Failure to attend or comply with the rules of the centre may result in:

- a fine of up to £1,000
- revocation and re-sentencing for the original offence (or committal to the Crown Court if that court made the original order). There are provisions analogous to those for other community orders whereby credit must be given to the extent that compliance has occurred, and allowing a custodial sentence to be imposed if the failure was 'wilful and persistent'.

SUPERVISION ORDERS

Orders placing offenders under the supervision of a local authority can be made in respect of young people below 18 years of age, usually by the youth court: see, generally, *Appendix F.*

AMENDMENT AND REVOCATION

There is provision for amending probation, community service, combination and curfew orders; and for the offender or supervisor to apply for revocation if there is a change in circumstances. Revocation can be ordered on its own, or coupled with re-sentencing depending on the circumstances. In some instances a subsequent court, on sentencing an offender to an immediate custodial sentence, can revoke an earlier order, but it has no power to re-sentence for the original offence in such circumstances. Attendance centre orders have their own statutory code for amendment and revocation. Seek further advice as necessary: 📖✋.

CUSTODY 📖✋

> **THRESHOLD CRITERIA**: there are three bases for using custody as follows:
>
> • the offence, or the combination of the offence and one or more offences associated with it, is so serious that *only* such a sentence can be justified (the 'so serious' test); or
> • the offence is a sexual or violent offence (both widely defined by the Criminal Justice Act 1991: but seek advice) and only such a sentence would be adequate to protect the public from serious harm from the offender (the 'protection of the public' test); or
> • following refusal to consent to a community sentence which requires such consent (or on breach of a community sentence for 'wilful and persistent' failure to comply with the sentence).

> **RESTRICTION ON LIBERTY**: the restriction on liberty resulting from custody is obvious—in that the offender is deprived of his or her physical freedom. However, the offender will normally be released under the scheme described in *Chapter 9* after serving part of his or her sentence.

Meaning of custody
Offenders aged 21 years of age and over are sentenced to a period of imprisonment. For those aged 18 to 20 years inclusive the order is for detention in a young offender institution—when the *minimum* sentence is 21 days (see page 62).

Associated offences
This has the meaning outlined in *Chapter 1*.

Imprisonable offences
The offence must be imprisonable. The statute which creates the offence will state whether the offence in question attracts imprisonment. Contrast a term of custody for failure to pay a fine (above) which can be ordered regardless of whether the offence itself carries imprisonment.

Procedural requirements
Before imposing a custodial sentence, the court must take into account:

- all of the information available to it regarding the circumstances of the *offence* or *offences,* including aggravating or mitigating factors.
- all of the information before it about the *offender* where custody or longer custody is being considered to protect the public from serious harm from an offender convicted of a violent or sexual offence.

'Sexual offence' and 'violent offence'—definitions
The 1991 Act lists those sexual offences to which the protection of the public ground for custody applies (the list covers most sexual offences—but not eg indecent exposure). Violent offences are widely defined so as to cover situations where an offence 'leads, or is intended or likely to lead' to death or physical injury (including arson). Protection from 'serious harm' means '. . . protecting the public from death or serious injury, whether physical or psychological'. Court advisers normally anticipate situations where definition is likely to be a live issue. 📖✋

Legal representation
There is a restriction on imposing custody (including a suspended sentence) where the offender is not legally represented after conviction and he or she is:

- under 21 years of age; or
- aged 21 or over and has never served a prison sentence (which does not include eg an unactivated suspended sentence, detention

in a young offender institution or committal for contempt or for non-payment of a fine).

The court should explain the effect of these provisions to an unrepresented defendant—with a warning to use the opportunity which the court is obliged to give by way of adjournment to acquire representation (if need be by applying for legal aid). Failure to obtain representation, to apply for legal aid, or refusal of legal aid on grounds of means will allow a subsequent court, if it considers it appropriate, to impose custody without the defendant being represented. An offender can waive these rights by declaring an unwillingness to consult a solicitor or to apply for legal aid—although it may be sensible to encourage him or her to consult the duty solicitor or probation officer before proceeding.

Pre-sentence reports
The court must obtain a PSR before deciding that either of the first two criteria for custody above (ie the 'so serious' test or the 'protection of the public' test) are made out—unless it deems a PSR to be unnecessary. Such a report is similarly needed in order to assess the appropriate length of the custodial sentence.

There is no comparable legal requirement for a pre-sentence report before deciding on a custodial sentence for failure to consent to a community sentence which requires consent, or for wilful and persistent failure to comply with such a sentence (see above)—although there will need to be evidence of the failure and other relevant circumstances.

Care must be taken as to what is said when calling for a pre-sentence report: see *Chapter 8*.

Length of custodial sentences
Custodial sentences take effect straight away (and, where there are two or more such sentences, concurrently to one another unless the court has specifically ordered that they take effect consecutively).

The seriousness of the offence or, as appropriate, the need to protect the public from serious harm from the perpetrator of a sexual or violent offence should determine the length of any custodial sentence within the maximum sentence available. The protection of the public criterion allows a sentence longer than would be justified by the seriousness of the offence in respect of a sexual or violent offence. Orders which are possible in the magistrates' court are as follows:

- imprisonment may be imposed for any period from a minimum of five days to the maximum available on summary conviction

(this is usually fixed by statute at from one month to six months per offence)
- periods can be ordered to take effect *consecutively* to:
  — previous sentences (ie those imposed on an earlier occasion)
  — other sentences passed on the same occasion subject to the following limits:
  (a) six months in aggregate; or
  (b) normally 12 months in aggregate where there are two or more either way offences
  — a suspended sentence which is being activated.

The same limits apply to detention in a young offender institution (ie so far as offenders in the adult age range of 18 to 20 years inclusive are concerned) but subject to a minimum sentence of 21 days, so that young offenders only receive custody if the offence warrants more than a nominal period.

Lord Bingham, Lord Chief Justice, has indicated that courts should explain to a defendant the effect of a custodial sentence taking account also of the early release provisions outlined in *Chapter 9.* 📖✍

Concurrent and consecutive sentences

Magistrates can order custodial sentences to be served concurrently to one another or consecutively (within magistrates' maximum powers: see under last heading). The decision is a judicial one. The court must state clearly whether sentences are concurrent or consecutive, for even stronger reasons with respect to the latter.

In practice, sentences are usually ordered to take effect concurrently unless there is a specific reason for them to be made consecutive. This will primarily depend on the court's assessment of the combined seriousness of the particular offences under consideration, or, as the case may be in sexual or violent cases, the extent to which there is a need to protect the public from serious harm from the offender. Case law suggests that custodial sentences may be made consecutive where eg the offences are of totally different types and/or are committed in separate incidents or whilst on bail.

Where an imprisonable offence has been committed during the operational period of a suspended sentence (below), the court should sentence for the new offence then decide whether to activated the suspended sentence. If so activated, this will normally be consecutive to any period of imprisonment imposed for the new offence.

Short local detention

Where imprisonment *is* an option, the offender may instead be detained within the precincts of the court or at a police station for any period up until 8 pm (typically until the court rises). The offender must not be deprived of the opportunity of returning home that day. None of the standard criteria, restrictions or prerequisites apply. The power only exists if the offender is 21 years of age or over. (Defendants aged 18 years upwards may however be placed in short local detention for fine default or contempt).

SUSPENDED SENTENCES

Imprisonment (but *not* detention in a young offender institution) may be suspended for between one and two years.

The court must first be satisfied that immediate imprisonment is appropriate, ie that the 'so serious' threshold has been reached. A suspended sentence should never be viewed as some lesser, or intermediate disposal. There must thereafter be 'exceptional circumstances' to justify suspension. Case law indicates that the following *cannot* be exceptional circumstances: previous good character, provocation, youth, early guilty plea, domestic difficulties, loss of career, long public service, the effect on pension entitlements (factors which should have been taken into account as personal mitigation before custody was settled upon). The Court of Appeal has interpreted the term 'exceptional circumstances' narrowly—although an example might be where an offender is in an extremely poor state of health.

Duty to consider a fine in addition
If the sentence of imprisonment *is* suspended the court must consider imposing, in addition, compensation and/or a fine.

Suspended sentences and probation
A probation order cannot be made at the same time as a suspended sentence of imprisonment, even in relation to a separate offence.

Commission of a further imprisonable offence
Conviction of *any* imprisonable offence *committed* during the operational period of a suspended sentence makes the offender liable to serve the sentence. He or she should be warned of this. If so convicted:

- the original period can be implemented for its full length (consecutively or concurrently to any imprisonment for the new offence: see also *Concurrent and consecutive sentences, above*). Implementation in full is compulsory unless the subsequent court considers that this would be unjust in all the circumstances, including the facts of the subsequent offence; or
- the original sentence can be implemented but reduced in length; or

- the sentence can be further suspended for up to two years; or
- the court can 'take no action'. This *is* a formal response. Courts should not take no action in the erroneous belief that the original court can still deal with the breach, particularly in the case of a Crown Court suspended sentence which magistrates cannot implement. They can either take no action or commit to the Crown Court (on bail or in custody) for it to consider the matter.

Suspended sentence supervision orders

The Crown Court can make a suspended sentence supervision order when it suspends *more* than six months' imprisonment for a single offence. Magistrates can commit to the Crown Court for sentence with this in mind (although the Crown Court may use immediate custody). The supervisor is a probation officer but supervision differs from that in a probation order. Failure to comply with the supervision element may result in a fine but not revocation and re-sentencing, nor activation of the suspended sentence. Only a further conviction can result in this. Such committals are nowadays relatively unusual: 📖✋

CUSTODY AND MENTAL DISORDER

Where the offender is or appears to be mentally disordered the court is obliged—in addition to the standard procedures for custody, above—to:

- obtain and consider a medical report from a registered medical practitioner approved for the purposes of the Mental Health Act 1983 unless it considers such a report to be 'unnecessary'
- in any event to consider all information before it relating to the offender's mental condition; and to
- consider what treatment may be available.

Chapter 10 provides further guidance on mentally disordered offenders.

REASONS FOR DECISIONS

When passing a custodial sentence magistrates must state in open court:

- that they are of opinion that either or both of the 'so serious' or 'protection of the public' grounds for custody apply; and
- why they are of that opinion.

They must also explain to the offender *in ordinary language* why they are passing a custodial sentence. These reasons are entered in the court register and specified in the relevant warrant. There is a duty to give extra reasons where the court passes a sentence for a sexual or violent offence which is longer than is commensurate with the seriousness of the offence. Again, this must also be explained in ordinary language. See also the need to explain the effect of the early release provisions: page 62. All such reasons and explanations must be valid in the judicial sense that they are properly relevant and supportable in law. Magistrates should, as a matter of good practice, check their intentions with the court adviser: 📖 🖐

EXAMPLES OF APPEAL RULINGS

The following summaries indicate how the Court of Appeal approached some early appeals following the Criminal Justice Act 1991:

- Although the 1991 Act did not define or quantify seriousness in comparative terms, an offence might be so serious that only a custodial sentence can be justified where, to borrow from pre-1991 case law, '. . . all right thinking members of the public, knowing all the facts, would feel that justice had not been done by the passing of any sentence other than a custodial one.': *R v Cox (David Geoffrey)* (1993) 14 Cr. App. R. (S.) 479.

- A short period of imprisonment (possibly 14 days) was appropriate for a motorist who in even a minor way assaulted another motorist in a dispute over driving: *R v Fenton* (1992) 13 Cr. App. R. (S.) 85. In another case, a sentence of six weeks was approved for a fairly similar offence: *R v Atkins* (1992) 13 Cr. App. R. (S.) 140.

- A short period of imprisonment (less than 28 days) was appropriate for a female ticket clerk on a ferry who went equipped to sell old tickets and thereby to deprive her employers of fares (only £4 was mentioned in the charges). This was a clear breach of trust by an employee who also did not receive credit for a guilty plea: *R v McCormick* (1995) 16 Cr. App. R. (S.) 134. In contrast, a custodial sentence was overturned and a community service order substituted when a 19-year-old shift manager in a pizza shop stole a total of £1,080 from his employers on three occasions, mitigating factors including his youth and immaturity being taken into account: *R v Small* (1993) 14 Cr. App. R. (S.) 404.

- Where a longer term of custody is justified to protect the public from serious harm from the offender, this consideration has to be balanced with the need to ensure that the sentence is not out of proportion to the nature of the offence: *R v Mansell* (1994) 15 Cr. App. R. (S.) 771.

The sentencing criteria in *Appendix B, Considerations Affecting Decisions Whether or Not to Commit to the Crown Court for Sentence* are based upon a range of Court of Appeal rulings. Judicial advice (*Chapter 11*) must keep abreast of such guidance and justices' clerks and other court advisers are responsible for drawing attention to key rulings, guideline judgments and, if appropriate, to rulings falling 'on either side of the line'—to assist magistrates in arriving at the correct sentence.

A Structured Guide to Sentencing

To be considered in conjunction with:

- the sentencing criteria in this chapter (and *Figure 1* on page 38)
- the Magistrates' Association Sentencing Guidelines: *Appendix C.*

NB Consideration of COMPENSATION pervades the whole sentencing process.

Consider the need for a PSR at appropriate points: *Chapter 8.*

Stage 1

DECIDE GUIDELINE LEVEL for an average offence of the type in question ie:

Level 1 Discharge
Level 2 Fine
Level 3 Community sentence
Level 4 Custody

Stage 2

REVIEW in the light of aggravating and mitigating factors affecting the
particular offence
MAKE INITIAL ASSESSMENT as to sentence level

Stage 3

Do previous convictions or responses to earlier sentences affect this initial
assessment? (see *Chapter 6*)
Was an offence committed whilst on bail?
REVISE ASSESSMENT as to level *if appropriate.*

Stage 4

CONSIDER whether, in certain situations, any matters concerning the
particular offender affect the sentence level: see pages 22, 32
REVISE ASSESSMENT as to level *if appropriate*
Arrive at FINAL decision as to which level applies.

Stage 5

CONSIDER sentence WITHIN the level selected.
Do any of the following serve to reduce sentence *within* the level:
Previous good character?
Other personal mitigation ('offender mitigation')?
Credit for a guilty plea?

Fines: Consider local guidelines and the defendant's individual financial circumstances and revise up or down as appropriate.

Community sentence: Consider 'restriction of liberty' and 'suitability'.

Custody: Consider length of sentence (noting the special rules for violent or sexual offences).

Whether or not considered at *Stage 3:*
Do previous convictions or responses to earlier sentences affect the above?
Is there an offence on bail?

Stage 6

MAKE SURE COMPENSATION HAS BEEN ADEQUATELY CONSIDERED

Stage 7

CONSIDER the TOTALITY PRINCIPLE
Is the final sentence still proportionate to the offence or offences?
If you have departed significantly from the guideline level at *Stage 1,* check the reasons for this.

Stage 8

Obtain any appropriate consent, agreement or indication of 'willingness.'

ANNOUNCE SENTENCE including any ancillary orders eg disqualification, endorsement, costs, forfeiture.
Give any statutory (or other appropriate) **REASONS/EXPLANATIONS** 📖✋

Note: *Always seek judicial advice before making a pronouncement in all but the most straightforward cases: see, generally, Chapter 11* 📖✋

Figure 2

Chapter 4

Compensation for Victims

The Court of Appeal has confirmed that the impact of a crime on a victim may affect the seriousness of the offence (*Attorney-General's Reference No 2 of 1995 (R v Summerfield)* (1996) 1 Cr. App. R. (S.) 274). Relevant information may be contained in the evidence, the prosecutor's outline, or any PSR (which should deal *inter alia* with the offender's attitude towards the victim: see *Chapter 8*). The term 'victim impact statement' is sometimes used to describe such information.

Quite apart from the fact that relevant factors may affect the sentence as such, payment of compensation by an offender to a victim is an overriding consideration in many cases. As indicated in *Chapter 2*, reparation—of which compensation is an aspect—is one of the general objects of sentencing. In practice, magistrates are required and encouraged to award compensation whenever possible. Two factors are important:

- sensitivity to the interests of victims; and
- the extent of the financial information about the offender.

Priority
Where both a fine and compensation *are* considered appropriate, but the offender's financial circumstances are not adequate to pay both in full, courts are required to give preference to a compensation order. It would thus be wrong to reduce the amount of compensation because of the defendant's financial circumstances and then to impose a fine as well.

Where compensation and a fine cannot both be imposed and where no additional form of sentence is considered necessary, compensation may be imposed as a sentence *in its own right*. Whenever it *is* coupled with another sentence compensation is described as an 'ancillary order'.

Loss, damage or personal injury
Where an offence causes loss, damage or personal injury, the court is obliged by law to consider whether the offender should pay compensation. Financial loss resulting, say, from a theft where the goods have not been fully recovered, or from criminal damage where items will necessarily have lost value is relatively easy to deal with provided that evidence of the amount of the loss or agreement by the defendant as to the value involved is forthcoming.

Personal injuries are less straightforward. Both medical evidence and legal advice may be needed. 📖 ✍ Personal injury includes physical or mental injury, so that, eg an award can be made for terror or distress caused by the offence. Thus in *Bond v Chief Constable of Kent* (1982) 4 Cr. App. R. (S.) 324 the High Court held that distress or anxiety directly arising from an offence could constitute 'personal injury' or 'damage' for compensation purposes. More recent cases have established, eg that assault can be committed without the use of direct physical force and that grievous bodily harm includes physiological injury (*R v Burstow*, *The Times*, 30 July 1996); and eg that physiological injury from an assault can even be caused by the use of words over a telephone (*R v Ireland*, *The Times*, 22 May 1996)—whilst statutes such as the Protection From Harassment Act 1997 seem specifically designed to pre-empt 'injuries' of this type.

Maximum amount

The magistrates' court limit is £5,000 per offence. But the court can order compensation for loss, damage or injury caused by offences which it has taken into consideration (TICs: *Chapter 2*), as well as those in respect of which it has actually convicted the defendant. The total is limited to the maximum the court could order for offences of which the offender stands convicted. If the offender is found guilty of, say, two offences and asks for seven others to be considered, the maximum compensation that can be ordered is £10,000 (ie 2 x £5,000).

Application

There is no need for an application to the court (although the prosecutor will often make one for the victim). The court *always* has power to make an award—provided there is sufficient information to enable it to set a figure: see also the reference to 'victim impact statements' (page 68) and *Contents of a PSR* in *Chapter 8*. If magistrates require better evidence of the loss, damage or injury, it is appropriate to ask the prosecutor to obtain this information (subject to the victim's own wishes).

Reasons

The court must give reasons if it decides *not* to make an order for compensation where there has been loss, damage or personal injury. The reasons must be announced in open court and be recorded in the court register.

Straightforward cases

Magistrates should order compensation in straightforward cases where the amount can readily be assessed. The power to award compensation in summary proceedings represents—in those cases where the offender's financial circumstances are sufficient to meet the award—a speedy means by which the victim can be reinstated. An award by magistrates avoids the prospect of a separate civil claim by the victim in the county court or High Court. See also *Fixing the amount*, below.

Road accidents

In most cases, compensation arising from road traffic accidents will not be ordered through the magistrates' court. However, an order can be made in respect of injury, loss or damage (other than that suffered by dependants as a result of death) due to an accident arising out of the presence of a motor vehicle on a road if it is in respect of:

- damage resulting from an offence under the Theft Act 1968 such as the unlawful taking of a motor vehicle (ie compensation may relate to the taken vehicle but not damage caused by it); or
- injury, loss or damage where
  — the offender is uninsured in relation to the vehicle; and
  — compensation is not payable under the Motor Insurers Bureau Agreement. This means that, in respect of property damage, the court is restricted to the first £175 of loss not covered by the MIBA (January 1998). But this may include any reduction in preferential rates (ie loss of no claims bonus).

Fixing the amount

When a court is considering a compensation order, it must satisfy itself that actual loss, damage or injury has resulted from the offence. The court will look at the cost of replacement or repair of goods damaged. Where items are of sentimental value it may be possible to draw common-sense comparisons with other property losses and the likely effect on the victim.

A court can consider loss of earnings following time off work due to a physical attack. It can also look at more intangible matters, such as pain, suffering and any loss of facility. Guidance contained in Home Office Circular No 53/1993 has, for the greater part, been adopted within the Magistrates' Association *Sentencing Guidelines* (for details see *Appendix C* to this handbook). The guidelines suggest awards for a range of injuries.

Usually prosecutor and defence will try to agree the value of any loss. Where there is a dispute, the court will normally hear evidence presented by the prosecutor who may decide to call the victim to prove the loss, damage or injury, or this may be proved by other evidence such as a receipt or a medical report. The offender may then make representations and/or call evidence. The matter need not be proved to the same standard as the offence in a criminal trial (ie beyond reasonable doubt)—but there must be some factual basis on which the court can arrive at a figure.

In *Bond v Chief Constable of Kent* (see page 69), the court stated that where a small sum was involved (£25 in 1982) the usual rule that the amount ordered had to be agreed or proved did not apply when considering anxiety or distress. The impetus behind this seems to be that common sense dictates that small amounts of compensation for real and obvious anxiety or distress occasioned by certain offending (eg a brick thrown through a house window, as in Bond's case) are permissible and should be encouraged. However, care must be taken if courts wish to consider large sums of compensation for major psychological problems said to be caused by offending: see *Straightforward cases*, above, and seek advice if necessary. 📖✋

Financial circumstances of the offender

Once the court is satisfied that there has been injury, loss or damage of a given value, its next obligation is to consider the offender's financial circumstances. It must have regard to these in so far as they appear or are known to the court. The Court of Appeal has interpreted this to mean that a compensation order should enable the offender to complete payment within a reasonable time, normally within 12 months. This can be extended to up to three years where the circumstances justify it. In many instances, the court will have required the offender to complete a financial circumstances form in relation to fines (*Chapter 3*). It cannot be over-emphasised that effective use of compensation often stems from the identification of financial resources which would enable the offender to meet an award—and giving compensation priority as required by law: see *Priority*, above.

In reaching its decision, the court may consider any savings or capital which the offender has and can also consider his or her expected income (often called 'potential income'). Where the offender can afford to repay only part of the value of the loss, then the court can and should order payment of that part.

Where there is a suggestion that an offender might be able to sell property (eg a car) to pay compensation it is important for a court to consider a proper valuation. The offender's valuation may be 'over-optimistic' or inaccurate—or there may be other considerations such as an uncompleted hire purchase or credit agreement.

Apart from minor differences, compensation is enforced in the same way as fines are (*Chapter 3*).

Compensation ancillary to a custodial sentence

If the offender is sentenced to a custodial sentence there are obvious difficulties. The court will need to consider whether the offender has or will have the means to pay the amount ordered. The Court of Appeal has indicated that it is wrong to make compensation orders which will be a burden on release from custody, as this may lead to further offences to raise the money to pay the order. It is also not generally appropriate to combine a compensation order with a substantial sentence of imprisonment unless immediate funds are available. If the sentence is short then there would seem to be nothing wrong in a court ordering compensation of an amount which would not be considered burdensome on release, eg imprisonment for three months and an order of compensation of, say, £200 to be paid by instalments.

Appeal and review

The victim's entitlement to receive any compensation ordered is suspended for 21 days to allow the defendant time to appeal, or until after any appeal is heard. However, enforcement of the order against the offender is *not* suspended, since the obligation to pay arises immediately. In circumstances where an appeal is successful, the court will have to return any monies already paid by the offender.

A court can also review a compensation order at some future date at the request of the offender, including where: a civil court has decided that the injury, loss or damage was less than the value placed on it by the magistrates' court; the property has been recovered; or the offender's means have deteriorated (seek advice as necessary 📖✋).

Choices for the victim

In theory victims can sue the offender for damages in the county court or High Court. Civil proceedings can be slow and expensive and an unwelcome further burden for victims. An order by magistrates provides the victim with a convenient and speedy remedy which avoids expense and delay—and represents a tangible expression of concern.

Typical decisions

Many decisions are straightforward and full compensation is ordered. However, from time to time, magistrates have to decide: whether to order any compensation at all; how much to order; how to balance competing claims of victims; and whether an offender with means should pay more than a joint offender without, eg:

(a) Offender A is long-term unemployed, on state benefit. He damages two plate glass windows value £1,000 each. The court has to decide how much compensation he can afford to pay by instalments out of his state benefit.

(b) Offenders B, C and D are charged with damage to property to the amount of £1,500. Offender B does not appear. A warrant is issued for arrest. Offender C enters a plea of guilty, is unemployed, in receipt of state benefit, and married. Offender D who has also pleaded guilty is single, working and earns £200 per week net. The Court has to decide whether offender D should pay the majority of the compensation or whether it should be apportioned evenly.

(c) Offender E, an adult, is being sentenced on a charge of assault occasioning actual bodily harm: an unprovoked attack on another motorist. The victim received two black eyes. The magistrates decide that in view of the nature of the offence and the offender's record, the sentence should be four months' imprisonment. They now need to consider the question of compensation to the victim. On the present guidelines, should they order the offender to pay about £200 compensation as well?

(d) Offender F, who is unemployed and in receipt of state benefits, pleads guilty to two charges of deception. The two separate victims are (i) an elderly pensioner, and (ii) a High Street bank. The pensioner has lost £600. The bank has lost £2,000. The magistrates need to decide whether the whole amount of compensation should be in favour of the pensioner rather than the bank, in view of the offender's limited financial circumstances.

GENERAL TREATMENT OF VICTIMS

In 1990, the government published a *Victim's Charter*. This outlined the reasonable expectations of victims and stated how victims should be treated by the various agencies. In consequence, there have been improvements in the support given to victims of crime and more sensitive treatment. Criminal justice services have also improved the extent to which victims are kept informed of the progress of a case and given the opportunity to provide information to decision-makers.

Victim Support

Victim Support (National Association of Victims Support Schemes) was formed in 1979. Each year, trained volunteers and staff based in nearly 400 local areas of England and Wales where schemes are in operation offer help to over one million victims of crimes ranging from burglary to the murder of a relative. This free and confidential service includes emotional support, practical help (eg with home security, and claims for insurance or criminal injuries compensation) and information. Victims are referred to schemes by the police, or make direct contact. Victim Support also runs the Witness Service, through which trained volunteers offer emotional support and practical information about court proceedings to victims, witnesses and their families before, during and after the trial. There are also services for defence witnesses in some areas. The Witness Service runs in every Crown Court and a growing number of magistrates' courts (expansion is dependent on identifying additional funding).

Victim Support also works to raise awareness of the effects of crime and to achieve greater recognition of victims' rights. There are over 16,000 volunteers and nearly 900 full-time and part-time staff. Victim Support is a registered charity, which receives a Home Office grant (£12 million in 1996-97).

Criminal injuries compensation

The Criminal Injuries Compensation Scheme, originally established in 1964, provides financial compensation to victims of crimes of violence and to those injured in attempting to apprehend offenders or prevent crime. The minimum award is currently £1,000 (January 1998) and injuries meriting lower awards cannot be compensated by the scheme. All applications are made to the Criminal Injuries Compensation Authority (CICA).

The payment of compensation for an injury as a result of a crime of violence is intended to be an expression of public sympathy and support for innocent victims. It is not, however, necessary for an offender to have been convicted before an award can be made. Under the scheme, injuries are classified into 25 bands ranging from £1,000 (eg for an undisplaced nasal fracture) to £250,000 (for paralysis of all four limbs). There are procedures for review, and in the event of dissatisfaction with the review, the possibility of an appeal to the Criminal Injuries Compensation Appeals Panel which has as its members lawyers, doctors and other people with relevant experience. The original application should normally be lodged no later than two years after the incident for which a claim is made.

Chapter 5

Other Orders of the Court

In addition to the four main levels of sentence outlined in *Chapter 3,* magistrates' courts possess a wide variety of powers to make other orders. This chapter deals with a range of powers which are not featured elsewhere in *The Sentence of the Court.* Generally, ▢👋.

BINDING OVER

Magistrates have power to bind over an individual to be of good behaviour and to keep the peace. The power—which stems in part from the Justices of the Peace Act 1361—may be exercised in the course of criminal proceedings without formal complaint. Accordingly it may be used at any stage of the proceedings when there are reasonable grounds for believing that there may be a breach of the peace in the future, eg disorder in court or a neighbour's dispute. A bind over under this ancient law is not dependent on a conviction and magistrates should normally seek advice where they are considering exercising this power of their own volition. ▢👋 A degree of caution may be necessary, eg if it is proposed that an acquitted defendant should be bound over.

The most usual way in which the power is considered is following a formal complaint by one person inviting the court to bind over someone else to keep the peace or to be of good behaviour pursuant to Section 115 Magistrates' Courts Act 1980. The alleged conduct must be capable of provoking violence and it must be unreasonable.

People aged 18 but under 21 may be detained and those aged 21 or over may be imprisoned should they refuse to enter into a recognisance to keep the peace or be of good behaviour. Any such detention or imprisonment will cease if the person concerned subsequently agrees to be bound over.

Most defendants *do* promise to behave and *do* enter into a recognisance, whereby they then incur the risk of forfeiting the sum of money to the Crown should they misbehave. The order is made for a period set by the court, often a year.

Following principles of natural justice, the defendant should always be told what is in mind and be allowed to address the court before any final decision is made. It is sufficient to establish a breach of the peace that the natural consequence of the conduct would, if persisted in, be to provoke other people to violence, so that some actual danger to the peace is established.

75

COSTS

Magistrates have power to award costs, subject to each case being dealt with on its merits. The basic rule is that costs can—and should normally—be awarded in favour of the successful party, including the Crown Prosecution Service. Costs must always be a reimbursement, ie they must not be used as a guise for punishment. Private prosecutors (eg the NSPCC, RSPCA, private individuals) may receive an order that their costs be paid out of central funds (public monies held by the justices' clerk), but not the Crown Prosecution Service or other public authority—since such organizations are funded out of the public purse.

Costs against offenders

The court can order a convicted offender to pay just and reasonable costs to the prosecutor. The amount must be stated in the order (and there is no power to refer taxation to the justices' clerk: compare a *Defendant's costs order,* below). An order should only be made where the court is satisfied that the offender has the means to pay. Costs cannot be ordered if the offender has been ordered to pay a sum not exceeding £5 (whether by way of fine or compensation)—unless the court, in the particular circumstances, considers it right to do so.

The principles governing time for payment of costs are similar to those affecting fines: see *Chapter 3.* It is wrong to order an offender to pay costs if he or she will be unable to pay within a reasonable time (usually, in practice, within 12 months).

Defendant's costs order

Where a case is dismissed, discontinued or withdrawn the court will usually make a defendant's costs order (sometimes called a 'DCO')—ie for payment of his or her costs from central funds (see above). Only exceptionally will a prosecutor be ordered to pay the defendant's costs instead, eg where the prosecutor was negligent in failing to deal with some aspect of the case which would have disclosed a sound defence at an early stage.

A defendant who is on legal aid will not receive a defendant's costs order in addition to the legal aid order, unless this is to recover expenses not covered by legal aid (eg travel to court).

A defendant's costs order is normally made following an acquittal or a case being discontinued by the prosecutor unless there are positive reasons for not doing so, eg where the defendant's own conduct has attracted suspicion and misled the prosecution into thinking that there was a strong case, or the defendant was acquitted on a technicality. Where someone is acquitted on some charges but convicted on others, the court has a discretion whether to make a defendant's costs order, or it might order only part of the defendant's costs. In this instance the amount must be specified by the court.

Unless the order is for an agreed or a part amount, the amount will be determined by the justices' clerk (as 'taxing officer') after the defence has submitted a detailed account.

Unnecessary or improper acts or omissions

Magistrates may order all or part of the costs to be paid by either party to the other (called an *inter partes* order)—irrespective of the final outcome of the case—if those costs have been incurred as a result of an unnecessary or improper act or omission, eg where a party forgets to warn a witness and the case has to be adjourned. Magistrates should seek advice. 📖✋

Wasted costs

Magistrates can disallow legal aid costs or order a legal representative to bear costs which are wasted. This means costs incurred as a result of any improper, unreasonable or negligent act or omission on the part of the legal representative. Magistrates should seek advice. 📖✋

RESTITUTION

Where goods have been stolen and someone is convicted of an offence relating to the theft, the court may order restoration of the goods to the person entitled to them (or of goods bought with any proceeds). Restitution can also be ordered on conviction for dishonest handling, obtaining by deception or blackmail. Goods include all property except land. An order can also be made in respect of TICs: see *Chapter 2*. An order can be made of the court's own volition (there is no need for an application) and may require:

- anyone having possession or control of the goods to restore them to a person entitled to them; or
- any other goods directly or indirectly representing the original stolen goods to be delivered to the person so entitled; or
- any money found on the offender not exceeding the value of the goods to be paid to that person.

The court may order restitution *and* compensation, eg if property is damaged—but restitution should only be ordered in clear cases. Magistrates should avoid trying to solve difficult questions of law.

DEPRIVATION AND FORFEITURE

When the offence consists of unlawful possession of property, the court may order the defendant to be deprived of that property. A deprivation order can also be made where property has been used to commit an offence or was intended to be so used, whether or not the defendant has been separately convicted of that other offence.

The court must be satisfied that the property has been lawfully seized from the offender, or was in his or her possession or control when apprehended, or when a summons was issued. An order can also be made in respect of TICs: *Chapter 2*.

'Property' does not include land. The court must have regard to its value and the likely financial and other effects of the order on the offender (together with any other order the court is contemplating). The effect of the order is to deprive the offender of the property—which passes into the possession of the police. This enables the true owner to make an application to the magistrates' court for an order for delivery up of that property. If there is no successful claim, the property will be sold and the proceeds disposed of at the direction of the court.

Where the offence results in someone suffering personal injury, loss or damage and the court has not been able to make a compensation order (*Chapter 4*) because of the defendant's lack of means, the proceeds of sale resulting from a deprivation order can be used as compensation.

If an offender is convicted of an offence under the Road Traffic Act 1988 which is punishable with imprisonment (such as driving whilst disqualified or an 'excess alcohol' offence), the vehicle used is, by law, to be regarded as having been used for the purpose of facilitating an offence. Thus, the offender may be deprived of the vehicle once the court has considered all relevant factors, including the value of the vehicle and the likely financial and other effects on the offender.

A deprivation order is appropriate only in straightforward cases where there would be no difficulty in implementation.

Many individual Acts of Parliament provide for forfeiture of specific items on conviction, eg the Misuse of Drugs Act 1971; Prevention of Crime Act 1953 (offensive weapons); Obscene Publications Act 1964 and Firearms Act 1968. In some cases the court can also order destruction or disposal of the item concerned.

CRIMINAL CONFISCATION ORDERS

In limited circumstances magistrates are able to make confiscation orders. They may confiscate the proceeds of certain offences, eg offences: relating to sex establishments; of supplying or possessing for the purpose of supply videos of unclassified works; and of failure to pay contributions under the Social Security Contributions and Benefits Act 1992. These procedures were established under the Proceeds of Crime Act 1995 and can be triggered by the prosecutor or by the court of its own volition. However, it will not normally be appropriate for the confiscation procedures to be invoked unless there is a realistic prospect of a confiscation order of £10,000 or more being made. Seek advice. 📖✍

EXCLUSION ORDERS

Magistrates' courts have power to make what are termed 'exclusion orders' in the following circumstances:

Licensed premises
This variety of exclusion order is designed for offenders who make a serious nuisance of themselves on licensed premises. Accordingly, such an order might not be appropriate eg for a one-off minor offence by a middle-aged first offender. The order is *additional* to the sentence for the offence (which could range from a discharge to custody). The effect of the order is to prohibit the offender from entering upon the licensed premises where the offence was committed or other specified premises without the consent of the licensee or someone acting on his or her behalf, such as member of staff.

'Licensed premises' means premises where a full justices' on-licence is in force (ie excluded are off-licences and registered clubs). The court must be satisfied that in committing the offence on licensed premises, the offender resorted to violence or offered or threatened violence.

It is open to the court to make an exclusion order of its own motion, ie without an application by the prosecutor or the victim. It is undesirable for application for such an order to be made by someone who is not a victim or party to the proceedings. The proper course for an interested third party to take is to make representations to the prosecuting authority.

The order may be for not less than three months nor more than two years. A copy is sent to the licensee of each specified premises—and as a matter of good practice to the local police. The licensee or someone acting on his or her behalf may then expel anyone who has entered or whom he or she suspects of entering the premises in breach of the order. A police constable must, at the request of the licensee or staff, assist in expelling anyone the constable suspects of such a breach.

Someone who enters premises in breach of an exclusion order is liable, on summary conviction, to a fine not exceeding Level 3 (£1,000) and/or imprisonment for one month. A court by which a person is convicted of a breach of the order must consider whether or not the exclusion order should continue in force—and may terminate or vary it

79

by deleting specified premises. An exclusion order is not otherwise affected by conviction for a breach of the order.

Football exclusion orders

Where someone is convicted of an offence connected with football, the court may make an exclusion order prohibiting him or her from entering any premises for the purpose of attending any prescribed football match. 'Offence connected with football' means:

- an offence committed at the ground or while entering or attempting to enter the ground in the two hours before the match, or leaving the ground up to one hour after it, provided the match is prescribed by the Home Secretary; or
- an offence involving the threat of violence or violence to a person or property or disorderly conduct or racial hatred on the way to or from any Association Football match; or
- an offence committed on the journey in breach of the Sporting Events (Control of Alcohol) Act 1985.

The court must be satisfied that the order would help to prevent violence or disorder at or in connection with prescribed matches. It must be for not less than three months (plus the unexpired period of any pre-existing order, or, if there is more than one such order, the most recent). An offender who enters premises in breach of an order commits an offence punishable by a Level 3 fine (£1,000) and/or imprisonment for one month. The offender may apply to terminate the order after it has been in force for one year.

An exclusion order can only be made in addition to a sentence for the offence of which the offender has been convicted. For these purposes absolute and conditional discharges (see *Chapter 3*) count as sentences. The court may, on the application of the prosecutor, order a constable to take a photograph of the defendant.

Under the Football Spectators Act 1989, courts dealing with an offender convicted of football related offences can make a 'restriction order' for a set period. This requires the offender to report to a police station at a time when a specified match is taking place *outside* England and Wales. The court must be satisfied that such an order will help to prevent violence or disorder at or in connection with designated matches. Agreements exist with Italy, Scotland, Sweden, Norway and the Republic of Ireland.

DISQUALIFICATION

Disqualification from driving is dealt with in *Chapter 7*. Magistrates may consider other types of disqualification in a variety of circumstances, eg in relation to:

Companies

Magistrates can make an order against an offender convicted summarily of an either way offence in connection with the promotion, formation or liquidation of a company, or with the receivership or management of its property, or a variety of offences in connection with company legislation (eg failure to file a return) prohibiting the offender, without the leave of the court, from being the director of a company or operating in other capacities within a company for a period not exceeding five years.

Animals

Magistrates have powers of disqualification in connection with various statutes dealing with animals, such as cruelty to animals where there is power to deprive someone of the ownership of the animal in question and to disqualify him or her from having custody of any animal. Legislation affecting pet shops allows magistrates in certain circumstances to disqualify an offender from keeping such a shop. Similarly, in respect of animal boarding establishments there is a power which enables magistrates to disqualify an offender from keeping such an establishment. Where someone is convicted of an offence in connection with the Dangerous Wild Animals Act 1976, the court may cancel any relevant licence held under that Act and may, whether or not the offender is the holder of such a licence, disqualify him or her from keeping any dangerous wild animal. In all cases, the period of disqualification is such as the court thinks fit.

Other disqualification orders

Other statutes cover such diverse topics as fishing licences, restaurant licences and gaming club licences. Under the Food Safety Act 1990, a court may prohibit the proprietor of a food business from participating in the management of any food business or any food business of a class or description specified in the order. There is also a provision within the Medicines Act 1968 which allows courts to disqualify an offender from using premises for a pharmacy for up to two years.

Notice

As a general rule, the defendant must after conviction and before sentence be given notice before any disqualification is imposed and an opportunity to make representations. Prosecutions for some of the above offences are fairly rare and advice is therefore essential: 📖🖐

DEPORTATION

Additional to the sentence for an offence punishable by imprisonment, the court may recommend to the home secretary that an offender who is not a British citizen, or a Commonwealth citizen having a right of abode in the United Kingdom, should be deported. The Home Secretary then decides whether or not to deport the offender. In coming to that decision, account will be taken of such factors as the nature of the offence, the length of stay in this country, previous convictions (if any), age, personal history, domestic circumstances and the strength of connections with this country. Any compassionate considerations and representations will also be taken into account. The Home Secretary is unlikely to deport a first-time offender unless the offence (allowing for any TICs) was particularly serious. This is a specialist area and legal advice should be sought, including in relation to European Community nationals to whom extra considerations apply. 📖 ✍

SEX OFFENDERS: POLICE REGISTRATION

Part I of the Sex Offenders Act 1997 imposes a requirement on offenders convicted or cautioned for specific sex offences to notify the police of their name and address and any subsequent changes thereto. The court issues a notice to this effect and gives it to the offender following conviction, certifying that they have been convicted of a qualifying offence. The court chairman will need to make an appropriate statement/explanation. Seek legal advice as to whether an offence is a 'qualifying offence' and concerning such an announcement. 📖 ✍

RESTRAINING ORDER: HARASSMENT

The Protection From Harassment Act 1997 creates two offences:

- a summary offence of causing harassment; and
- an either way offence of putting a person in fear of violence.

When sentencing someone convicted of either offence, the court can make an order restraining the defendant from future acts of harassment. This order can be made for a specified period or until further order. A breach of such an order is itself a separate, either way offence.

The expectation is that the prosecutor will invite the court to make the order, taking account of what is necessary for the victim's or other people's protection. A restraining order can be varied in the future, but can only be made at the time of the original sentence. It is not the prosecutor's duty to apply for the order, merely to remind the court of its existence. As a restraining order is ancillary to sentence, a right of appeal (including against the restraining order) exists.

Restraining orders can *only* be made following a conviction under the 1997 Act.

Chapter 6

Previous Convictions and Responses to Sentences

It is part of the regular practice of the magistrates' courts for prosecutors to submit lists of previous convictions once someone stands convicted of an offence: *Chapter 2*. The relevance of the information contained in such lists turns on the true meaning of section 29 Criminal Justice Act 1991. This entire subject is one where legal/judicial advice may be desirable in an individual case. 📖 ✋

The original section 29 attracted sufficient criticism for the government to announce its replacement within eight months. The revised section 29 governs the place in the sentencing process of:

- previous convictions; and
- responses to previous sentences.

It seems clear, irrespective of any legal rules, that if an offender has previous convictions, particularly if they are for similar offences, then this reduces the extent to which he or she can put forward mitigation. The offender cannot claim to have a 'clean record'. Similarly, if eg earlier community sentences have not been complied with this says something about the suitability of such sentences now: see, generally, *Chapter 3*. But section 29 goes further.

The original section 29

As indicated in *Chapter 1*, an intention of the 1991 Act was that courts should pass sentences proportionate to—ie 'commensurate' with—the offence or offences of which the offender stands convicted. The original version of section 29(1) thus provided that:

> An offence shall not be regarded as more serious for the purposes of any provision of [the sentencing provisions of the 1991 Act] by reason of any previous convictions of the offender or any failure of his to respond to previous sentences.

Section 29(2) then stated that:

> Where any aggravating factors of an offence are disclosed by the circumstances of other offences committed by the offender, nothing . . . shall prevent the court from taking those factors into account for the purpose of forming an opinion as to the seriousness of the offence.

83

Thus, whilst previous convictions or responses could not affect the seriousness of the present offence, the facts of other offences which actually shed light on the current offence so as to make it more serious could. It was these provisions that attracted such widespread criticism.

Common law principles prior to section 29 CJA 1991

Unpopular as section 29 was, there were those who thought that it merely set out the principle that an offender should not be sentenced for offences for which he or she had already been punished. The approach adopted by courts until 1991 was that whilst previous convictions might restrict or eliminate the mitigation which could otherwise reduce a sentence (above), a criminal record could not justify a more severe sentence, one *disproportionate* to the seriousness of the present offence.

Confirmation of the validity of such views can be found in the comments of the late Lord Taylor of Gosforth, Lord Chief Justice, in an address to the Annual General Meeting of the National Association for the Care and Resettlement of Offenders (NACRO) in 1993. Lord Taylor suggested that common law rules laid down by the Court of Appeal before 1991 should still be regarded as valid.

Section 29 today

In introducing the present provision into Parliament, the then Home Secretary stated that the original version had:

> ... unnecessarily fettered the hands of the courts and imposed a strait–jacket on their ability to sentence justly in individual cases.

The present section 29(1) reads:

> ... in considering the seriousness of the offence, the court may take into account any previous convictions of the offender or any failure of his to respond to previous sentences.

The change of emphasis is clear. But it is not entirely obvious exactly how the provision alters the court's approach. In the public statement already referred to, Lord Taylor went on to say:

> I believe that the philosophy of the Criminal Justice Act 1991 as it was originally envisaged still holds good. I believe though, that the amendments [ie the new Section 29] have improved it and have made it more realistic.

Certainly, a defendant with no previous convictions might claim that the offence was less serious because it stemmed eg from 'a foolish, spur of the moment decision by someone with an otherwise unblemished record', whereas such convictions would, to the extent that they were relevant to the situation under consideration, limit or eradicate the scope for mitigation. It is less clear to what extent previous convictions can increase (or 'aggravate') the seriousness of the present offence. Following basic principle, it seems that they ought not to be used to justify a sentence wholly *disproportionate* to that offence.

The relevance of past incidents

The new section 29 does not mean that *all* previous matters are capable of affecting the seriousness of an offence, and magistrates should always consider the relevance of previous incidents when sentencing for a new offence. They should also be conscious about how much emphasis to place on the offender's record when deciding upon seriousness. The Magistrates' Association *Sentencing Guidelines* (see *Appendix C* to this handbook) offer the following advice:

> Take care in using previous convictions or any failure to respond to previous sentences in assessing seriousness. We recommend that courts should identify any convictions relevant for this purpose and then consider to what extent they affect the seriousness of the present offence.

Thus even where previous convictions or failures to respond to previous sentences of the court might affect the seriousness of an offence the question must always be answered 'To what extent?'

Court of Appeal guidance

Commentators on section 29 have expressed concern that it is now easier for the courts to send minor offenders into custody. It is correct to say that prior to the original version of the 1991 Act (page 83) imprisonment was sometimes a response to persistent minor offending and could not be justified by the seriousness of the present offence (see *Sentencing Practice in the Crown Court*, Home Office Research Study No 103, 1988). One general message from the Court of Appeal is that there are some offences which do not pass the seriousness threshold/test for custody, notwithstanding that the offender may have a long list of previous convictions for similar offences. Thus, eg where a woman, already on a suspended sentence for burglary used a false instrument and obtained property by deception and was sentenced to three months' imprisonment for theft of bacon valued at £3.50 from a shop, the Court of Appeal stated that notwithstanding the breach of the suspended prison sentence, and a background of previous offending, the offence did not justify imprisonment: *R v Wendy Bond* (1994) 5 Cr. App. R. (S.) 430. This suggests that there is a 'seriousness ceiling' for some offences which cannot be exceeded simply because of previous convictions.

Previous responses

An aspect of section 29 on which there has, as yet, been no comprehensive judicial guidance is the impact of the phrase 'response to previous sentences'. At first sight, it is difficult to understand how failures to respond to earlier sentences *can* affect the seriousness of the present offence. One view is that the provision refers to *any* conduct following the imposition of the earlier penalty. Another is that it refers to breach of an existing sentence or a further offence committed during that sentence: see *Chapter 3*.

Summary

If an offender has previously been convicted of other offences, or has failed to respond to previous sentences, this could rarely be taken into account under the original section 29. The Criminal Justice Act 1993 introduced a new approach. Courts *are* now permitted to consider the offender's record when assessing the seriousness of the present offence or offences—but must adopt a careful approach in assessing the relevance of previous convictions or responses to seriousness. There are areas needing clarification by the Court of Appeal eg:

- should a court take previous matters into account if they are similar in type and/or recent, but not if they are different in type and/or were committed a long time ago?
- to what extent *can* previous convictions affect the seriousness of a new offence, ie does the current offence set a 'seriousness ceiling' and/or is the correct rule that sentence should not become wholly disproportionate
- does a failure to respond to previous sentences include sentences which were completed without a breach or merely sentences which were breached, or still current at the time of a later offence?
- what is the precise connection between previous responses and the seriousness of the present offence?

It should be noted that previous convictions may be relevant to the 'protection of the public' test for custody in relation to *sexual* or *violent* offences for entirely different reasons. Unlike the 'so serious' test, the 'protection of the public' test involves an assessment of future risk (ie of serious harm to the public). Relevant past offences may be an important indicator of the extent of that risk.

Chapter 7

Road Traffic Offences[1]

In addition to any penalty, certain motoring offences attract endorsement of the offender's driving licence or disqualification.

ENDORSEMENT

For many traffic offences, the court *must*, by law, order that the defendant's driving licence is endorsed with:

- particulars of the offence, and
- the number of 'penalty points' appropriate to that offence.

The only exception is where a court finds '*Special reasons' for not endorsing:* see below. If no licence is held, the order operates as an order to endorse any licence which the offender obtains.

Penalty points

Every endorsable offence carries a number of penalty points, from a minimum of two to a maximum of eleven. Some of the more common offences and their points are:

Careless or inconsiderate driving	3-9
In charge (offences relating to alcohol/drugs)	10
Failing to stop after an accident	5-10
Failing to report an accident	5-10
Driving whilst disqualified	6
Using etc. a motor vehicle whilst uninsured	6-8
Driving other than in accordance with a licence	3-6
Exceeding a speed limit	3-6
Failure to provide a preliminary specimen for a breath test	4
Failing to comply with traffic lights/directions	3
Construction and use offences	3
Contravention of pedestrian crossing regulations	3
Using a vehicle in a dangerous condition	3

Appendix D contains a list of all endorsable offences and their points. The chief significance of the system of penalty points lies in the 'totting up' provisions described under *Obligatory disqualification* below.

---

[1] For a useful outline of this everyday topic, see *Introduction to Road Traffic Offences* (Waterside Press). Available from May 1998.

Variable points

Where an offence carries a range of points, the court has a discretion concerning the number to be endorsed—which will depend on the court's view of the seriousness of the offence.

Where someone is convicted of two or more offences *committed* on the same occasion, the number of points to be endorsed is usually the highest number attracted by any one of the offences. Thus eg if an offender is convicted of driving while disqualified (six points) and contravening pedestrian crossing regulations (three), then six points would be endorsed. Instead of following this general rule, courts may add the numbers together, making nine points in the example given. However, the court is obliged to give reasons if it adopts this course. The reasons must be announced in open court and be recorded in the court register. Seek advice if necessary: 📖 ✋.

'Special reasons' for not endorsing

As already indicated, when someone is convicted of an endorsable offence, the court *must* order endorsement and the relevant number of points unless it decides—on the basis of evidence—that there are special reasons for not doing so. The court must state in open court any grounds for finding special reasons, and these must be entered in the court register. A special reason means:

> a mitigating or extenuating circumstance, not amounting to a defence in law, but directly connected with the offence and which the court ought properly to take into account.

Special reasons must relate to the *offence,* as opposed to the *offender.* So, if the offender puts forward the fact that he or she was hitherto of good character and had driven for many years without being convicted of any offence, this would not amount to a special reason in law—since it relates to the offender. The onus is on the offender to establish special reasons and he or she must prove them on a balance of probabilities. If the licence is not endorsed, no points are imposed. Seek advice if necessary: 📖 ✋

Additionally and quite separately to special reasons, there is a procedure with construction and use offences (eg defective brakes, tyres, steering) whereby endorsement can be avoided if the offender establishes that he or she did not know of and had no reasonable cause to suspect the defect. Seek advice if necessary: 📖 ✋

Special reasons and appeals

Where the offender is aggrieved by a decision to order penalty points despite his or her assertion that special reasons exist, there is a right of appeal to the Crown Court or to the High Court on a point of law. The prosecutor also has a right of appeal to the High Court if it is contended that the magistrates' decision on this issue is wrong in law.

Penalty points and fixed penalties

Where an offender has accepted a fixed penalty (below), there is no court hearing. If the offence carries a range of points (such as speeding, ie 3-6) the number of points imposed is the lowest in the range.

DISQUALIFICATION FROM DRIVING

Disqualification can involve the application of complex legal rules. Generally speaking, advice is desirable: 📖 🖐. There are two types of disqualification.

Discretionary disqualification

The power to disqualify an offender at the court's discretion exists *whenever* an offence is endorsable. A court considering discretionary disqualification should, as a matter of natural justice, warn the parties what is in mind. A discretionary disqualification may not be imposed for the same offence if the offender is also liable to be disqualified under the penalty points provisions (see *'Totting up,'* below), and will not usually arise where the offence is subject to an *Obligatory disqualification*.

Obligatory disqualification

Obligatory (or 'mandatory') disqualification arises due to:

- the nature of the offence; or
- the cumulative effect of earlier disqualifications; or
- most frequently in practice under the totting up provisions.

Offences for which the offender must be disqualified
There are several offences for which an offender *must* be disqualified (usually for a minimum of a year):

- driving/attempting to drive whilst unfit through drink or drugs
- driving/attempting to drive with 'excess alcohol' in the blood or urine
- failing or refusing to provide a specimen for analysis after driving
- dangerous driving
- aggravated vehicle taking.

In all cases, the court *must* order the defendant to be disqualified for 'such period not less than twelve months' as it thinks fit—unless the court for special reasons (ie relating to the offence) thinks fit to order the offender to be disqualified for a shorter period, or not to order a disqualification at all.

The principles affecting special reasons have already been set out in relation to endorsement above—including the requirement to state the grounds for finding any such reasons in open court.

Cumulative effect of earlier disqualifications

A magistrates' court *must* impose a minimum disqualification of two years on an offender on whom more than one disqualification for 56 days or more has been imposed within three years immediately preceding the commission of the offence—if the offence of which he or she has now been convicted involves obligatory disqualification.

This means that an offender who is convicted of any of the offences listed under the heading *Obligatory disqualification* above and who has, within three years immediately preceding the commission of that offence, been subject to more than one disqualification for a period of 56 days or more, must be disqualified for at least two years.

Along similar lines, where an offender is convicted of a drink/driving offence *committed* within ten years of a previous conviction for such an offence, the minimum period of disqualification is not one year but three—unless the court decides, for special reasons, to reduce this obligatory disqualification, or not to impose one at all: and see also *Length of totting up disqualification*.

'Totting up'

In the main, the penalty points system is aimed at the offender who persistently commits relatively minor offences, and who ought to be disqualified because of repeated disregard for the law. Where a driver accumulates 12 or more points within a three year span, he or she must generally be disqualified for a minimum period (usually called a 'totting up' or 'penalty points' disqualification). In totting up, the points to be taken into account are:

- those falling to be endorsed for the offence before the court; and
- any that were endorsed on a previous occasion for offences committed within three years of each other, unless already 'wiped clear' by disqualification under the penalty points system (ie previous totting up).

When a court disqualifies the offender under the totting up provisions, no penalty points are endorsed for the current offence.

Length of totting up disqualification

The minimum period of a totting up disqualification is:

- *six months* if no previous disqualification falls to be taken into account; or
- *one year* if one previous disqualification falls to be taken into account; and
- *two years* if more than one previous disqualification falls to be taken into account.

A previous disqualification falls to be taken into account if it was imposed within three years of the latest offence which brought the offender's points total to 12. It need not have been for totting up (it could have been for an offence involving obligatory disqualification such as drink driving). However, it must have been for 56 days or more and must not have been imposed for stealing a motor vehicle, taking without consent, or going equipped for theft.

'Mitigating circumstances'
Under the totting up provisions, the offender must be disqualified for one of the minimum statutory periods set out above unless the court is satisfied that there are grounds for mitigating the normal consequences of conviction and sees fit to disqualify for a shorter period, or not to disqualify at all. The onus of establishing mitigating circumstances is on the offender—on a balance of probabilities. No account may be taken of:

- triviality of offence
- hardship, other than 'exceptional hardship'
- circumstances previously taken into account within the three year period.

Mitigating circumstances must not be confused with special reasons (see page 88). Mitigating circumstances are far wider in scope—and, in the ordinary way, they will mainly refer to the *offender*. The exceptional hardship put forward will usually relate eg to loss of livelihood if disqualification is imposed. If this plea succeeds and the court reduces the minimum period, or decides not to disqualify, then the offender cannot put forward the same ground again until three years have elapsed. Since mitigating circumstances must be announced in open court and are recorded in the court register, courts can make enquiries as to what grounds were found at an earlier hearing.

Under the penalty points scheme only one disqualification is imposed irrespective of the number of offences. In the event of an appeal against any one or more of the offences, the disqualification will be treated as having been imposed in relation to each endorsable offence. The Crown Court has power to alter sentences imposed by magistrates for several offences, even if the appeal only relates to one of them.

Theft, taking vehicles without consent and similar offences

The general rule is that there can be no discretionary disqualification unless the offence is endorsable. But courts may impose disqualification in respect of offences of taking a motor vehicle without consent, stealing a motor vehicle or going equipped for the theft of a vehicle—despite the fact that these offences are not in themselves endorsable.

The rule against consecutive disqualifications

Disqualifications cannot be imposed on the same or a subsequent occasion to run consecutively to each other.

Disqualification in absence after notice

An offender cannot be disqualified in his or her absence without first being given the opportunity after conviction of attending an adjourned hearing. As an alternative, the court may issue a warrant for the arrest of the defendant (always seek legal advice: 📖✋).

Commencement of disqualification

Disqualification starts from the moment it is imposed (credit being given by the DVLA for any interim disqualification: see under next heading).

Interim disqualification

Where the court has power to impose an immediate disqualification after conviction it also has power to impose an interim disqualification if:

- committing the defendant to the Crown Court for sentence
- remitting to another magistrates' court for sentence
- deferring sentence: see *Chapter 2*.
- adjourning after conviction.

Accordingly, when eg a magistrates' court adjourns after conviction for a pre-sentence report (see generally *Chapter 8*), or a DVLA print-out (ie a computer record of the licence), it may impose an interim disqualification. The DVLA will reduce by the period of the interim disqualification the length of any disqualification imposed by way of sentence at the end of the case. An interim disqualification will automatically last until the case is finalised but, in any event, will not last for more than six months and the court has no power to make a repeat order for the same offence.

'Rehabilitation schemes'—reduced disqualification

Where a defendant is convicted of driving or being in charge when under the influence of drink or drugs, or driving or being in charge with excess alcohol in the blood or urine, or failing to provide a specimen, and is disqualified for a period of not less than 12 months, the court has power to *reduce* the period of disqualification by three months, or where it is for a longer period than 12 months by a period of not more than one quarter of its length—provided that the defendant agrees to participate in a rehabilitation course. Such an order can only be made where:

- the court is satisfied that a place on a course is available
- the offender appears to be 17 years of age or older
- the effect of the order is explained to the offender and that he or she is required to pay the fees for the course before it begins, and
- the offender consents to the order being made.

If the offender completes the course successfully and pays the fees involved, a 'certificate of completion' will be forwarded to the court and the reduced disqualification will take effect. Rehabilitation courses are only available in certain areas of the country as at the time of writing.

Disqualification until a test passed

When a court convicts an offender of any road traffic offence—for which disqualification is obligatory or discretionary—it can order the defendant to be disqualified until he or she passes a driving test. As long as there is no other disqualification in force, the defendant is entitled to drive a car but must display 'L-plates' and be supervised. If he or she drives without L-plates or supervision, then a charge of driving whilst disqualified can be brought.

The Court of Appeal has repeatedly emphasised that this type of disqualification is not intended as a punishment—but is to protect the public against incompetent drivers or those who fail to use their driving skills properly. Accordingly, the prime reason for considering such an order is the interests of road safety. Orders will generally be in respect of offenders who, through age, infirmity or the circumstances of the offence, display incompetence. Any court disqualifying someone for a long period of time and having misgivings about the offender's ability when the period expires may wish to also consider imposing a disqualification until the offender passes a test.

When the court convicts an offender of dangerous driving, it is not only obliged to disqualify the offender for a minimum of one year—but it must also order disqualification until a test is passed: the 'extended driving test'. This test is longer and more rigorous than the standard 'L-test', and takes place in a variety of road conditions.

When an offender is convicted of an offence involving obligatory disqualification, or is liable to totting up, and the court, in its discretion, decides to order disqualification until the offender passes a test, then the test taken by the offender is the extended driving test.

Removal of disqualification

Anyone who has been disqualified (except eg for an interim period or until they have passed a test) can apply to the court for the removal of the disqualification and, if successful, disqualification may be lifted from a date specified in the order. The offender may apply:

- if the disqualification was for less than four years, after two years
- if the disqualification was for less than ten years but not less than four years, when half the period has elapsed
- in other cases, when a period of five years has elapsed.

If the application is refused, the offender must wait at least three months before reapplying. The court should have regard to the character of the offender and his or her conduct subsequent to the offence, the nature of the offence and any other circumstances. The provisions do not differentiate between *discretionary* and *obligatory* disqualification. Many applications concern three year disqualifications for a second drink/driving offence inside ten years. The offender can apply for the return of his or her licence after two years; but case law indicates that magistrates will need a lot of convincing before removing a disqualification which an earlier court was obliged by law to impose.

Disease or physical disability

There is a mandatory provision of the Road Traffic Offenders Act 1988 whereby—in any proceedings for an offence committed in respect of a motor vehicle—it appears to the court that the defendant is suffering from any disability or prospective disability, such as is likely to cause his or her driving of a vehicle to be a source of danger to the public, to notify the Secretary of State. There must be sufficient material before the court, eg something said by way of mitigation suggesting that the defendant is suffering from a relevant disability or a prospective disability. However, actual conviction is not necessary. Accordingly, a court might use this provision eg in respect of a defendant acquitted of careless driving because of a 'dizzy spell', or in respect of someone who is suffering from mental disorder and who is made subject to a hospital order without being convicted (see *Chapter 10*). The Secretary of State has various powers including to revoke the licence.

Fine default

From 1998 the government intends to empower certain courts to use disqualification from driving for fine default. Seek advice locally: 📖 ✍

A NOTE ON FIXED PENALTIES

The time, trouble and expense involved in court proceedings can be avoided for some motoring offences by the police offering the alleged offender a fixed penalty ticket. This offer can be accepted by payment of the fixed sum—when that is the end of the matter. If the matter is not dealt with in this way, then the usual result is a prosecution and court hearing in the normal way.

The fixed penalty system extends to a range of motoring offences, from simple parking to some that carry endorsement such as speeding, pedestrian crossing and construction and use offences involving tyres, steering and brakes. Where there is a range of penalty points (see above) and the fixed penalty procedure is used, the lowest number of points in the range is endorsed on the driving licence. The offer of a fixed penalty is a matter entirely for the police. The procedure depends on whether the offence is endorsable or not.

Offence not endorsable

A police constable (here a traffic warden may perform the duties of a constable) hands a fixed penalty ticket to the driver or, if the driver is absent, attaches it to the vehicle. The defendant has to pay the fixed penalty within 21 days to the relevant justices' clerk (or within such longer period as is allowed by the ticket). The amount (as at the time of writing) is normally £20, unless the offence is illegal parking in London, when it is either £30 or £40 depending on the circumstances. If payment is made within the time limit, that is the end of the matter. If not—and no court hearing is requested—the police may serve a 'notice to owner' upon the registered keeper of the vehicle. This provides a fresh opportunity for the fixed penalty to be paid. If it is not paid, various things can happen:

- the person served may request a hearing (proceedings then commence in the normal way); or
- the person served may satisfy the police by means of a statutory statement of ownership that he or she was not the owner of the vehicle at the material time. He or she will then escape liability altogether; or
- if not the driver when the offence occurred, he or she can furnish a statement of ownership together with a statutory statement of

facts countersigned by the actual driver. This will enable the police to prosecute the identified driver, if they wish to do so.

Driver present—endorsable offence

The officer requires the driver to produce his or her driving licence. Assuming that the driver is not liable to a totting up disqualification (above), the constable can offer the alleged offender the option of a fixed penalty and invite him or her to surrender the licence. If the driver does not have the licence with him or her, the constable may issue a provisional fixed penalty notice. The driver then has seven days to produce the notice plus the missing driving licence at any police station. If he or she does this and it is confirmed that no totting up disqualification is due, the offender will be given a fixed penalty ticket from that police station.

Requesting a hearing

Whenever there is an offer of a fixed penalty, the defendant can, within the stated time limit, ask for a court hearing. Proceedings are then conducted in the normal way, with the defendant being invited to plead guilty or not guilty.

Non-payment of a fixed penalty

If the penalty is unpaid at the end of the period allowed by the ticket, the fixed penalty (£20 non-endorsable offences and £40 endorsable offences) plus 50 per cent of this amount will be registered for enforcement as a fine at the defaulter's home court.

Conditional offer of fixed penalty

A conditional offer scheme is available for all fixed penalty offences (including those which carry endorsement). This allows the police to issue a notice by post to the registered keeper of the vehicle requiring information as to the identity of the driver.

The conditional offer of a fixed penalty is issued to the person identified by the registered keeper as the driver on the occasion when the offence was detected. Should the keeper fail to give information as to the identity of the driver, he or she commits an offence which is itself endorsable. If the driver wishes to take up the offer, he or she will send his or her driving licence and payment to the fixed penalty clerk named in the notice. He or she will accept payment subject to the driver's licence not disclosing that a totting up disqualification is due.

This relatively new procedure is being phased in—initially only in relation to offences detected by automatic devices.

DVLA PRINTOUTS

After conviction and before sentence for any road traffic offence carrying endorsement, the court should obtain either the defendant's driving licence or a printout of the defendant's driving record. Printouts are necessary in all cases where the defendant's licence cannot be obtained—or one has not been issued. They are obtained from the Driver and Vehicle Licensing Authority (DVLA), Swansea, and contain details of any endorsable offences that an individual has been convicted of and a note of any driving disqualifications. The printout also shows the sentences and court details.

Some courts operate a 'magnetic tape interchange' whereby they put the information onto a magnetic tape via computer, then post the tape to the DVLA which transcribes it and sends back the relevant printouts. Many courts are considering the introduction of landline links to further improve services. This means that the period of any adjournment can be kept short. In other instances, it normally takes about three to four weeks to obtain a printout. However, where a defendant appears before the court in custody, then rather than delay sentencing, a designated officer of the court can apply for an expedited printout by telephone. This will be transmitted to the court by facsimile.

REVOCATION OF NEW DRIVER'S LICENCE

The Road Traffic (New Drivers) Act 1995 came into effect in 1997. A main object of the Act is to reduce the level of accidents and injuries amongst newly qualified drivers. This is achieved by mandatory revocation *by the DVLA* of a driving licence where a new driver accumulates *six or more* penalty points on his or her driving licence within two years beginning with the day on which he or she first passed a test to drive any class of motor vehicle. He or she is then only entitled to hold—and drive in accordance with—a provisional licence until they have passed a re-test.

Although the court does not order the revocation, as a matter of good practice the licence holder should be advised by the court that the penalty points imposed will lead to revocation under the Act. Once notified by the court, the DVLA will send a revocation letter to the defendant which will take effect from 5 days after the date of issue. The 1995 Act is intended to introduce a road safety measure and magistrates should be alert to the fact that some defendants may encourage them to impose a short disqualification to circumvent that legislation. A short disqualification (which will not result in *any* penalty points being endorsed on the licence or notified to the DVLA) may be more attractive to the defendant than a re-test.

Chapter 8

Pre–sentence Reports

A central decision-making tool in relation to more serious offences is the pre-sentence report or 'PSR'. Prior to the Criminal Justice Act 1991, courts used reports prepared by the probation service or social services—known as 'social enquiry reports'. The 1991 Act renamed these and introduced a more structured approach. At the same time, the preparation and content of reports became subject to a Home Office/Probation Service 'National Standard for Pre-sentence Reports'.

BASIC PRINCIPLES

A pre–sentence report is a report *in writing* which:

(a) with a view to assisting the court in determining the most suitable method of dealing with an offender, is made or submitted by a probation officer or by a social worker of a local authority social services department; and

(b) contains information as to such matters, presented in such manner, as may be prescribed by . . . rules made by the Secretary of State.

The National Standard mentioned above has served for item (b). Standard adjournment periods for post-conviction PSRs—usually of three weeks—should be agreed and included in local *Statements of Preferred Practice* (see later in this chapter). When it is in the interests of justice, expedited PSRs can be prepared during shorter adjournment periods, or even, in appropriate circumstances, on the same day.

The obligation to consider a PSR

The court *must* consider a PSR when contemplating a custodial sentence or certain types of community sentence: see *Chapter 3*. However, this rule was relaxed in 1993 so that there is now a general discretion to dispense with a PSR if the court dealing with a given case deems one to be 'unnecessary'. Sentences are not invalidated by the failure of the court to obtain a PSR—although any court on an appeal against sentence must obtain a PSR if one was not obtained by the court below (subject to the same discretion to deem a report unnecessary). For all practical purposes, the former strict legal requirements have thus been replaced by good sentencing practice—which dictates that a PSR is appropriate whenever a court is considering any of the more severe forms of sentence unless the report could have no real effect on the court's decision. Where magistrates have power to commit for sentence to the Crown Court (see *Chapter 2*), no requirement is placed upon them to order a PSR even though they will have arrived at a decision to commit because of a feeling that their own powers of punishment are insufficient. Apart from this exception, the situations in which the potential sentence can be predicted with certainty in the magistrates' court are rare. Since the law was amended by the Criminal Justice and Public Order Act 1994, the following are practical examples of when a PSR *may* be declared unnecessary, ie where a defendant is:

- already serving a custodial sentence and a further custodial sentence is envisaged
- already serving, or has just completed, a community sentence and is reported as suitable for a further such order
- where the offence is so obviously very serious that the court would find it impossible to contemplate any other option. (This last example may, however, be more likely to occur in the Crown Court).

In cases where a PSR is obtained, it forms part of the relevant information which a court should consider before deciding on such important matters as the seriousness of the offence or offences, restriction of liberty and suitability for a particular community order. Among other things, PSRs contain information about what demands will be made on the offender by a given sentence. PSRs are also relevant in relation to the risk of the offender re-offending—both generally and, more particularly, in relation to the protection of the public from serious harm from the offender where the court is dealing with a sexual or violent offence.

PREPARATION OF THE REPORT

Once a PSR is ordered and an adjournment allowed for it to be prepared, the report writer will aim to produce a report which is impartial, balanced and factually accurate. The writer will bear in mind that *prima facie* the report is for the court. However, from 1 April 1998 it is intended that certain prosecutors will automatically be entitled to receive a copy of the PSR, whilst the decision whether to disclose to other prosecutors will depend upon an exercise of discretion by the court.

It is important to note that a PSR does not represent the interests of any individual or organization. The report writer will provide a professional assessment of the case—including the nature and the cause of the offence or offences and a note of any action which can be taken to reduce re–offending.

The National Standard confirms that a PSR must always be provided if requested by a court; this despite the fact that an offender might refuse to assist in its preparation. The writer will aim to produce the most useful report possible, ensuring that the offender was offered at least two opportunities for an appointment. The writer will, in any event, take all reasonable steps to obtain available, relevant information about the offender and his or her circumstances. If applicable, this should include the fact that the offender has said that he or she would, or would not, wish to carry out a particular community sentence. In such circumstances it remains for the court to decide whether to impose the community sentence in question, except in those few cases where consent remains a legal requirement (see page 50).

CONTENTS OF THE PSR

To accord with the National Standard, a PSR should be clear, concise, free of jargon, coherent and accurate in grammar, syntax and spelling. It will start by setting out basic information on a front sheet, following which information will appear under the following main headings :

- an introduction
- offence analysis
- relevant information about the offender
- an assessment of the risk to the public of re–offending
- a conclusion (including in appropriate instances a proposal).

The purpose of a PSR is clearly defined:

> . . . to provide a professional assessment of the nature and causes of a person's offending behaviour and the action which can be taken to reduce re-offending.

The introduction
This will include a summary of the sources drawn upon to prepare the report, identify steps taken to verify information and, if appropriate, draw attention to any other potentially useful sources to which it was not possible to have access. If the writer is doubtful about any information, this will be noted. The report should also state whether the offender is known to the writer, the probation service or social services, and the number of interviews undertaken in preparing the report. Any *lack of access* to specific information, eg previous convictions or

100

information from the Crown Prosecution Service should always be clearly recorded.

Offence analysis

This will normally include:

- an analysis of the offence or offences, including an assessment of the offender's culpability and the degree of premeditation
- information about aggravating or mitigating features of the offence which might assist the court when assessing seriousness (the PSR will not actually use the terminology of aggravation or mitigation)
- an assessment of the context of the offence, including information about any relevant associated offences
- a note of the offender's motivation, with the aim of helping the court to understand why the offender committed the offence or offences
- an assessment of the consequences of the offence ie the actual damage, injury, harm, cost of the offending (including the impact on the victim: see next point and, generally, *Chapter 4*)
- an assessment of the offender's attitude to the victim, the offence, awareness of its consequences, any expressed remorse or guilt and any desire to make reparation and/or provide compensation
- an assessment of any special circumstances eg family crisis, alcohol, drugs, physical or mental health directly relevant to the offending. The report will draw attention to ways in which these might be relevant to 'seriousness'
- where there is a specific feature of the offence which seems to conform to a pattern of previous offending (eg targeting vulnerable victims) this should be included.

Seriousness of the offence

As part of the offence analysis, the report writer will form a view about how serious the offence is—so as to ensure that the restriction of liberty contained in any proposed community sentence is commensurate with the offence. The writer will be steered by any initial indications of seriousness given by the court. This is discussed more fully on page 103.

Information about the offender

This part of the report is critically relevant when assessing the suitability of particular community orders for the offender; and to his or her attitude towards the relevant offence or offences and the victim or victims—and also towards particular sentencing options. It summarises the offender's personal and social circumstances and evaluates any patterns of offending identified in the light of the personal or social factors which have contributed to them. This part of the PSR covers offending history and deals with issues of relevance to section 29 Criminal Justice Act 1991 with regard to previous convictions or failures to respond to earlier sentences (see, generally, *Chapter 6*). The assessment should refer to positive *and* negative results, eg successful completion of earlier sentences, breach of an order, or a further offence committed whilst subject to a previous community sentence. Partial successes on which future sentences might build are also highlighted. Ultimately, the report will give a balanced picture of the offender, including both favourable and unfavourable items, and should note any positive action taken by him or her since the offence was committed.

The desirability or otherwise of a medical or psychiatric report (see *Chapter 10*) is also covered. If appropriate, the report writer will invite the court at the earliest opportunity to consider ordering one. Whilst the National Standard does not make reference to the point, it is good practice for the report writer to endeavour to liaise with the author of the medical report when preparing the PSR, otherwise there is a risk of the two reports being at odds with one another.

Risk to the public of re-offending

The report writer will consider the risk of re–offending and the risk of harm to the public, including the risk of serious harm in relation to any sexual or violent offences for which a more severe or longer sentence might be passed (*Chapter 3*). This risk element has two dimensions—the nature and seriousness of possible future offences, and the likelihood of their occurring. It should be noted that defence advocates might sometimes object to what they see as 'speculative' views expressed in a report, or question the evidence upon which predictions are based.

The conclusion

The conclusion in the PSR should flow logically and directly from the rest of the report. The National Standard indicates that unless the offence is 'so serious' that a custodial sentence is inevitable, or not 'serious enough' for a community sentence, this part of the report should propose a community order which contains a degree of restriction on liberty matching the seriousness of the offence. Where the conclusion indicates that a programme can be arranged, the report should contain a proposal and invite the court to consider its merits. If not, the report should make it clear that a programme cannot be proposed, and why. Where the proposal envisages a probation order, any non-standard requirements (often called 'additional requirements') should be set out in the terms proposed.

Where the PSR envisages a probation order or combination order, it should contain an outline of the proposed supervision plan. When community orders are proposed, there should eg be a description of the purposes and desired outcomes, the methods to be used, a timetable with targets for achieving objectives, a note of the proposed frequency of contact with the offender, of when community service work will take place, and the likely effect on other members of the family. The description of any proposed programme should indicate the degree of restriction of liberty involved, how the disposal will help tackle the behaviour which led to the offence and the steps to be taken if the offender does not comply. Where a community sentence requiring consent is proposed (see page 50), the report should always state whether or not the offender appears to be willing to comply; whilst in every case the defendant's motivation in relation to a particular community sentence will be a relevant consideration for both the Probation Service and the court.

Unless the court has specifically asked for the report to cover a number of options, any proposal will be for a single sentence—an explanation being given in appropriate cases if other options have been considered and rejected.

Where custody is likely, the report should identify matters which might have adverse effects on the offender and his or her family, and any considerations relating to length of sentence.

CONFIDENTIALITY

Reports are confidential documents and the information in them is limited to what is relevant to the sentencing process. (A point which remains valid even when a prosecutor is allowed sight of a PSR: see above under *Preparation of the Report*). When a custodial sentence is passed, a copy of the order is normally sent to the probation service/social services department in the custodial institution to assist in the sentence and release arrangements (as outlined in *Chapter 9*).

The content of the PSR is brought to the attention of the offender by the report writer. This may mean reading it out in private for those who cannot read; including having an interpreter read and translate it to an offender whose first language is not English. A copy of the PSR is given to the offender and to his or her legal representative.

INITIAL INDICATIONS OF SERIOUSNESS

It assists a report writer in preparing a satisfactory PSR—and gives him or her a starting point—if, when adjourning for a PSR, some initial indication of seriousness is given by the court. Conversely, it may not lead to the most effective analysis if the court merely announces that it wishes to keep all its sentencing options open. Such vague statements became prevalent following cases such as *R v Gillam* (1980) 2 Cr. App. R. (S.) 267 where it was held that if a court requests a report to ascertain, say, an offender's suitability for community service, then if the report shows that the offender *is* suitable, the court should not impose a more severe penalty—otherwise a sense of injustice might arise.

It is often suggested that the court should aim to give the report writer an indication of the court's preliminary view but without creating in the mind of the defendant any specific expectations—which might not be fulfilled even eg if an offender *is* deemed suitable for some form of community sentence. Thus the court should not restrict itself in any way concerning its final decision—when it comes to impose sentence—*after* it has considered *all* relevant information, including that contained in the PSR.

Courts approach this difficult aspect of their responsibilities in different ways and practices vary. Magistrates should check the local arrangements, any probation service protocols/understandings and any local suggested court pronouncement and explanations. 📖✋

RESPONDING TO A PSR

The PSR writer must consider the interests of the public as well as those of the offender. Sentencing is ultimately the responsibility of the court and there will be times when it declines to follow even a well reasoned PSR. There should be no need for any discord as between the court and the PSR writer if both have followed correct practice and proper procedures.

STATEMENTS OF PREFERRED PRACTICE

National Standards require that each probation area should develop a Statement of Preferred Practice for each magistrates' court in its area. Statements are usually drawn up between the chairman of the bench and the justices' clerk and local probation service (in consultation with social services). They may set time targets for the preparation of PSRs and afford priority to the situation where an offender is in custody awaiting sentence.

Statements of preferred practice need to cover not only the preparation of PSRs but to set out an agreed basis of requirements and expectations as between the probation service and the local court. Because they are a two-way agreement they should, wherever possible, be followed. In that way such agreements contribute to the efficient administration of justice particularly if they are available in court for reference purposes.

A NOTE ON NATIONAL STANDARDS

'National Standards for the Supervision of Offenders in the Community' were first introduced by the Home Office, Welsh Office and Department of Health in 1992 and a revised version was published in 1995. HM Inspectorate of Probation measures satisfactory compliance with the standards. In relation to PSRs, a stated aim is to strengthen the service provided to courts by:

- building upon the skill and experience of practitioners
- enabling professional judgment to be exercised within a framework of accountability
- encouraging the adoption of good practice
- setting a priority on the protection of the public
- establishing the importance of considering the effect of crime on victims.

More generally, the standards set out what is required of probation staff and social workers, providing a framework for good practice, accountability and achievement.

Outline of the Early Release Scheme

- Prisoners serving less than 12 months are released automatically at the half-way stage of their sentence (sometimes called **AUTOMATIC UNCONDITIONAL RELEASE (AUR)**). They are eligible for voluntary after-care, and can be returned to prison by a court for the rest of the existing term (ie in addition to any prison sentence for the new offence) if they are convicted of a further imprisonable offence during this period.

- Prisoners serving 12 months to under four years are subject to **AUTOMATIC CONDITIONAL RELEASE (ACR)**

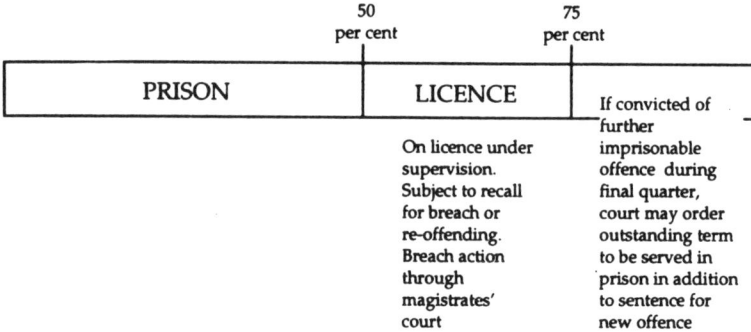

- Prisoners serving four years and above are subject to **DISCRETIONARY CONDITIONAL RELEASE (DCR)**

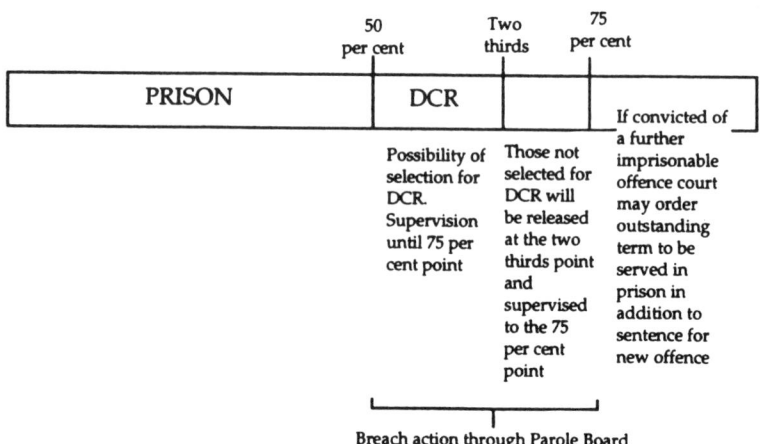

Figure 3

Chapter 9

The Early Release Scheme

A parole system for the release of prisoners has been in force in England and Wales since 1968. The Parole Board dealt with questions affecting release—and under the then system of remission, prisoners (other than those serving a life sentence) were released from prison free from any restrictions after serving two–thirds of their sentence. It was also possible for an offender to be released on parole after serving one third of his or her sentence. The system was in need of overhaul, partly because of the disparity between the sentence imposed and the actual time served.

The Criminal Justice Act 1991 thus introduced the scheme described in this chapter and summarised in *Figure 3* on page 106—and the Crime (Sentences) Act 1997 added to the earlier provisions. Lord Bingham, Lord Chief Justice, has indicated that courts should explain to a defendant the effect of a custodial sentence taking account of these provisions. 📖✍

Release on licence
All prisoners sentenced to imprisonment for 12 months or more are placed on licence on release until the three–quarters point of their sentence (though sex offenders may be on licence until the end of their sentence). Released prisoners are normally supervised by a probation officer as a condition of the licence (or if the person released on licence is under 22 years of age the supervisor can be a local authority social worker). The scheme applies equally to detention in a young offender institution.

Early release of short-term prisoners
Prisoners serving less than four years ('short term prisoners') must be released as soon as they have served one half of their sentence. If the sentence is for less than 12 months the prisoner is released *unconditionally* (ie not on licence)—usually referred to as 'automatic *unconditional* release' (AUR). If the sentence is for 12 months or more, but less than four years, the prisoner is released on licence subject to conditions—'automatic *conditional* release' (ACR).
In all cases, additional days' imprisonment ordered as punishment for misbehaviour in prison are added to the portion to be served before the offender is released.

107

Early release of long-term prisoners

Prisoners serving four years or more must be released as soon as they have served two-thirds of their sentence, but can be released on licence at the half-way point—usually called 'discretionary conditional release' (DCR). In either case, the licence expires at the time when the prisoner would have served three-quarters of his or her sentence.

Additional days imposed for misbehaviour are added to the portion to be served before the offender is released.

ENFORCEMENT

Enforcement has two main objectives:

- to secure compliance with the licence; and
- to recognise cases where this cannot be achieved and take action.

Throughout, the need to protect the public is a primary concern.

Breach of licence condition by short-term offenders

A short-term prisoner who fails to comply with the conditions of his or her ACR licence is liable on conviction in the magistrates' court to a fine not exceeding Level 3 (£1,000 at the time of writing). In addition, the court may, whether or not it passes another sentence for a fresh offence, suspend the licence for a period not exceeding six months and order recall to prison for the period for which the licence is suspended. A pre-sentence report (PSR) is not required by law (but may be desirable in some instances). If not present, the offender is liable to be detained and presumed to be unlawfully at large. (There is no power to issue a warrant, or a need for one).

Breach of licence by long-term prisoners

The Home Secretary has power to revoke the licence and recall the offender to prison if recommended to do so by the Parole Board. If it appears expedient, the Home Secretary may do this without such a recommendation—but the Board must be informed.

Commission of a further offence

A court convicting a prisoner—long-term or short-term (including an AUR prisoner, released from a sentence of under 12 months)—of an imprisonable offence committed following early release but before the 'face value' of the original sentence has elapsed may, whether or not it passes a prison sentence for the new offence, order the offender to be returned to prison for all or part of a period equal to whatever period of the original sentence remained on the day the offence was committed.

108

The court has this power whether or not the conviction for the new offence occurs before or after the date on which he or she would have served the full sentence but for the early release. Magistrates' powers are limited to six months, but magistrates can commit to the Crown Court for sentence. The period can be ordered to be served before or concurrently with any sentence for the new offence. A PSR is not required (but may be desirable in some instances).

The procedure to be adopted when a magistrates' court deals with the commission of a further offence has caused difficulties and has led to a number of reported cases, including the ruling of the Court of Appeal in *R v Taylor (Adrian Edward)*, *The Times*, 11 August 1997. When dealing with such matters seek advice: 📖

LICENCE CONDITIONS

Every licence contains standard conditions designed to facilitate its operation. Extra conditions may be imposed to prevent offending, ie:

- to attend upon a. duly qualified psychiatrist, psychologist or medical practitioner for such care, supervision or treatment as that practitioner recommends
- not to engage in any work or other organized activity involving a person under a specified age
- to reside at a specified place and not to reside elsewhere without the prior approval of the supervising officer
- not to reside in the same household as any child under a given age
- not to approach or communicate with a specified person or persons without the prior approval of the supervising officer
- to comply with requirements imposed by the supervising officer to address problems relating to alcohol, drugs, gambling, sex offending, solvent abuse, anger, debt or offending generally.

Breach of any of these extra licence conditions has the effect already described above.

ROLE OF THE PROBATION SERVICE

The probation service works in co–operation with the prison service to carry out supervision of prisoners before and after release. The aims of this work are:

- protection of the public;
- prevention of re–offending; and
- successful reintegration into the community.

The work is governed by a 'National Standard for the Supervision of Offenders by the Probation Service Before and After Release'.

RESIDUAL PAROLE BOARD FUNCTIONS

Since 1991, the Parole Board plays a more limited role, principally in relation to long-term prisoners and 'lifers'. The Board advises the Home Secretary on matters referred to it which relate to the early release or recall of prisoners. The Board also deals with the discretionary conditional release (DCR) of offenders serving four years or more.

A note on life sentence prisoners
The Board has power to direct the home secretary to release a prisoner who is serving a *discretionary* life sentence or a *mandatory* (ie automatic) life sentence for an offence other than murder. Where, however, the prisoner is serving a life sentence, or custody for life, *for murder*, the Board may recommend early release but here the final decision lies with the home secretary. Unless impracticable, the Board will be consulted when the home secretary is considering releasing a life sentence prisoner on licence or on compassionate grounds.

HOME CURFEWS

As at the time of writing, the forthcoming Crime and Disorder Bill will include new provisions for selected non-violent prisoners nearing the end of their sentences to be released early subject to 'home curfew' enforced by electronic tagging. These provisions are unlikely to be implemented before October 1998 at the earliest.

Chapter 10

Mental Disorder

In addition to its standard sentencing powers a magistrates' court has jurisdiction to make the following orders:

- a *hospital order* whereby someone is detained for medical treatment until discharged
- a *guardianship order* whereby someone is placed under the guardianship of a social services department or an approved person.

In all cases the maximum sentence available on conviction by magistrates must include imprisonment. The court need not have convicted the defendant (due to his or her mental state) but it must be satisfied that he or she committed the act or made the omission alleged by the prosecutor. The court must have considered medical reports from two doctors who are in agreement as to the defendant's mental condition (one of whom must be approved for this purpose pursuant to the Mental Health Act 1983). It must also be satisfied that any necessary arrangements for admission to hospital have been made.

Before such orders are made, the court may remand the defendant on bail, in custody, or, where appropriate, to a hospital for reports to be produced. Following these being obtained, an interim hospital order can be made until the court is satisfied as to the correct disposal.

If a magistrates' court feels that there should be a restriction placed on the date of release from hospital, it may commit the defendant in custody to the Crown Court for an *order restricting discharge* to be attached to any hospital order made by that court.

All the above matters are further explained below. Advice is recommended, generally: 📖🖐

DIVERSION FROM THE CRIMINAL PROCESS

Attempts are made to divert people away from the criminal courts if they are suffering from mental disorder and where treatment is considered to be more appropriate than punishment.

Many magistrates' courts are involved in such arrangements, which include duty psychiatrist schemes and multi–agency liaison to ensure that medical personnel are in attendance or on call. The arrangements stem from Home Office Circular 66/1990, 'Provision for Mentally

Disordered Offenders'. The Crown Prosecution Service also endorses the spirit and objectives of the circular in its own Code of Practice.

In 1997 the Mental Health Unit of the Home Office undertook a survey to try and obtain a clear and accurate picture of inter-agency arrangements throughout England and Wales and to produce a comprehensive breakdown of schemes and projects which are on offer. The main findings were that there is very considerable inter-agency activity around the country; but there is a wide variety in the composition, role and function of those groups.

INSANITY

If an accused person is brought before a court for a criminal offence, he or she may raise the defence of insanity. If this succeeds, he or she is liable to be detained at Her Majesty's pleasure, ie indefinitely. The defence is, therefore, in practice, confined to serious offences in the Crown Court where the consequences of conviction may be a very long sentence.

SENTENCING IN THE ORDINARY WAY

If a mentally disordered person is capable of being dealt with by the court and is found guilty, all normal sentencing options apply, including a probation order with a condition of medical or psychiatric treatment: see *Chapter 3*. Mentally disturbed offenders cannot be committed to prison simply because of their mental condition—ordinary sentencing principles apply as with every other defendant. However, if a court is considering custody for a mentally disordered offender, the law obliges it to obtain a psychiatric report before making that a decision.

SPECIAL PROVISIONS

The law gives the courts special sentencing powers where a defendant pleads guilty or is found guilty of an offence—for which the maximum penalty on conviction by magistrates includes imprisonment—and where he or she is in need of psychiatric treatment and suffering from one of four categories of mental disorder defined in the Mental Health Act 1983. The orders in question are hospital orders and guardianship orders: see below.

Orders made without a conviction

In summary cases, if magistrates are satisfied that the accused did the act or made the omission charged, they may, in the circumstances below, make a hospital or guardianship order *without* convicting the accused.

Even if the offence is triable either way (see *Chapter 1*) and the accused is unable, because of his or her mental condition, to indicate a plea or consent to summary trial the same procedure applies and an order may be made. The circumstances referred to above are as follows:

- the court must first be satisfied that the offender did the act or made the omission with which he or she is charged, ie the physical element of the offence (known as the *actus reus*) as opposed to the mental element (*mens rea*)
- the court must be satisfied on the written or oral evidence of two registered medical practitioners (one of whom must be approved for the purpose) that the offender is suffering from mental illness, or psychopathic disorder, severe mental impairment or mental impairment as defined in the Mental Health Act 1983. This will be by a psychiatrist (but note that both psychiatrists and chartered psychologists can provide treatment under probation orders)
- the court must be of the opinion, having regard to all the circumstances, including the offence, antecedents, and other available methods of disposal, that the most appropriate method of disposal is the order under consideration
- when making a hospital order, the court must be satisfied on oral or written evidence that arrangements have been made for the offender to be admitted to a specified hospital within 28 days.

HOSPITAL ORDERS

The effect of a hospital order is that the offender is admitted to hospital and detained there—initially for 12 months or until discharged by the hospital authorities or a Mental Health Review Tribunal. The court may give directions for the offender to be detained in a suitable place until he or she can be admitted to the hospital.

Courts have sometimes experienced difficulty when arranging for mentally disordered offenders to be admitted to hospital—either for a full hospital order or an interim hospital order (below). One reason for this has been the large increase in demand for what the Department of Health calls 'medium secure beds'—brought about by the substantial increase in the number of prisoners transferred to hospital under Mental Health Act provisions. There is planned development within the National Health Service capital programme to provide further beds. In the meantime, a named senior officer in each Regional Health Authority can be contacted by telephone—the aim being to assist the court by finding an appropriate placement as expeditiously as possible.

Orders restricting discharge

Where the Crown Court makes a hospital order, that court may also make a restriction order if this is considered necessary for the protection of the public. The order restricts release for a specified, or indefinite, period. In practice, restriction orders are for more serious offences—and cannot be made by magistrates' courts.

If magistrates consider that the accused is likely to commit further offences if at large, then having regard to the nature of the offence and the antecedents of the offender, they may commit him or her in custody to the Crown Court for a restriction order to be made.

Interim hospital orders

If a hospital order might be appropriate the court has power to make an interim hospital order, ie where it is not sure whether to make a full order straight away or deal with the offender in some other way.

Before making an interim order the court must be satisfied that all necessary arrangements have been made for admission to the hospital (in this situation *within* 28 days). Interim orders last for a maximum period of 12 months. At the end of the period of the interim order the court may make a full hospital order or deal with the offender in some other way.

GUARDIANSHIP ORDERS

Guardianship orders place the offender under the guardianship of a local authority social services department or of some person approved by the local authority. The purpose of such an order is to enable patients to receive community care where it cannot be provided without the use of compulsory powers. Someone who is subject to a guardianship order is not liable to be detained. Treatment cannot be given without consent.

Guardianship orders may be particularly suitable in helping to meet the needs of mentally impaired offenders who could benefit from occupation, training and education in the community.

The pre–conditions for making guardianship orders are essentially the same as for hospital orders (above). Orders remain in force for an initial period of six months but may be renewed. The effect of such an order is to give the guardian power to require the patient to live at a specified place, to attend places at specified times for medical treatment, occupation, education or training and to allow access by a doctor, approved social worker or other specified persons.

REPORTS

Before making either a hospital order or guardianship order the court must receive and consider appropriate reports (including, where applicable, a PSR) and be satisfied, in the case of a hospital order, that the necessary arrangements have been made for admission to a hospital. In addition to its ordinary powers to remand on bail or in custody the court has two further powers: to remand the offender to a hospital for a report on his or her mental condition if the court is satisfied by written or oral evidence that arrangements have been made for admission to a specified hospital within seven days; or to make interim orders (above). In summary:

- the defendant must be remanded (ie kept in custody for up to three weeks or released on bail for up to four weeks)
- conditions attached to bail ensure co-operation with the preparation of reports
- if the offender is *in custody*, the prison will arrange for the reports
- if the offender is *on bail*, the court (often with the help of a probation officer, who will usually be requested to write a co-ordinated PSR) will make the arrangements
- only a 'duly qualified medical practitioner' can prepare the report
- special scales of fees are paid by courts for reports.

Mental disorder is a complex subject and it is essential that defendants are legally represented whenever possible. Equally, it is advisable for magistrates to seek advice. 📖✋ The outline provided in this chapter represents no more than a basic introduction, sufficient to familiarise readers with the core issues.

Chapter 11

Judicial Advice

Sentencing has become more complex in recent times, due mainly to an increasing amount of legislation. This has created a range of new offences and introduced fresh rules, procedures and sentencing considerations. Whilst sentencing takes place within the framework outlined in this handbook, there are often further legal and judicial considerations. Courts are also required to give valid reasons or explanations for a range of sentence-related decisions.

LAW, PRACTICE AND PROCEDURE

The law in relation to sentencing is found not only in Acts of Parliament and Statutory Instruments (SIs), but also in rulings of the Court of Appeal (Criminal Division) and the High Court. These courts interpret sentencing legislation and occasionally give general guidance.

The Court of Appeal has emphasised that its decisions in relation to appeals against sentence—see the examples of case summaries on page 65—serve as examples of how a particular offender ought to have been dealt with in relation to a given offence. What are known as 'guideline judgments'—ie rulings which deal with sentencing issues in a more general way—are clearly of greater import than an isolated appeal ruling. Many rulings of the higher courts are contained in law reports,[1] whilst any significant developments are noted in the regular legal journals.

In addition, non-binding guidance on a range of matters is issued by ministers of the Crown acting within their particular fields of responsibility. Thus, the home secretary is responsible for criminal policy, including the development of legislation affecting the sentences available to the courts. Home Office circulars—issued to courts and others—outline the official stance. Established practice in an area or

---

[1] These are validated/recognised accounts which can be cited in court for or against a given proposition. Magistrates may occasionally encounter a 'transcript', normally where the proceedings of a higher court have gone 'unreported'. Lawyers/advisers are trained to discern the higher court's 'reasons for deciding' (or *ratio decidendi*: often shortened to *ratio*) and to apply the reasoning to the facts of future cases; also to recognise what is *binding* and what is merely *persuasive*.

locality is also something which affects the way in which sentence decisions are arrived at.

It is the responsibility of advisers to magistrates to be conversant with such items—and particularly with current developments. They are all professionals who receive special training in this regard. Their specialities include criminal law, evidence, procedure, sentencing and the principles of judicial decision-making.

THE JUSTICES' CLERK

The justices' clerk—as legal and judicial adviser to the bench—is under a duty to ensure that magistrates receive all appropriate advice. The justices' clerk's duties are set out in statute and augmented in a *Practice Direction* issued by Lord Lane when Lord Chief Justice. The relevant parts of that direction are reproduced overleaf. On a day to day basis, his or her responsibilities may be discharged by other qualified staff usually nowadays called 'legal advisers' (formerly 'court clerks') although, increasingly, the term 'judicial adviser' is heard—which is arguably a more exact description given the broad nature of their responsibilities to magistrates charged with making not just legal but judicial decisions.

The main duties of the justices' clerk (and other advisers) are to fully acquaint magistrates with matters relating to law, practice and procedure relevant to the latters' duties in or out of court. The key statutory provision states:

> . . . it is hereby declared that the functions of a justices' clerk include the giving to the justices to whom he is clerk, or any of them, at the request of the justices or justice, advice about law, practice or procedure . . . including questions arising when the clerk is not personally attending on the justices or justice and the clerk may, at any time when he thinks he should do so, bring to the attention of the justices or justice any point of law, practice or procedure that is or may be involved in any question so arising.

The independent nature of this duty is reinforced by the Justices of the Peace Act 1997 under which the justices' clerk—and the professional staff who discharge his or her functions on a day to day basis—are shielded, in individual cases, from any form of direction, from whatever source, when carrying out any responsibilities which have a judicial context.

The Practice Direction
The role of the justices' clerk/legal adviser is nowhere better encapsulated than in a *Practice Direction* given by Lord Lane in 1981:

Magistrates' Courts — The Role of the Clerk

1. A justices' clerk is responsible to the justices for the performance of any of the functions set out below by any member of his staff acting as court clerk and may be called in to advise the justices even when he is not personally sitting with the justices as clerk to the court.

2. It shall be the responsibility of the justices' clerk to advise the justices as follows:
   [a] on questions of law or of mixed law and fact;
   [b] as to matters of practice and procedure

3. If it appears to him necessary to do so, or he is so requested by the justices, the justices' clerk has the responsibility to:
   [a] refresh the justices' memory as to any matter of evidence and to draw attention to any issues involved in the matters before the court;
   [b] advise the justices generally on the range of penalties which the law allows them to impose and on any guidance relevant to the choice of penalty provided by the law, the decisions of the superior courts or other authorities.

   If no request for advice has been made by the justices, the justices' clerk shall discharge his responsibility in court in the presence of the parties.

4. The way in which a justices' clerk should perform his functions should be stated as follows:
   [a] the justices are entitled to the advice of their clerk when they retire in order that the clerk may fulfil his responsibility outlined above.
   [b] Some justices may prefer to take their own notes of evidence. There is, however, no obligation upon them to do so. Whether they do so or not, there is nothing to prevent them from enlisting the aid of their clerk and his notes if they are in doubt as to the evidence which has been given.
   [c] If the justices wish to consult their clerk solely about the evidence or his notes of it, this should ordinarily, and certainly in simple cases, be done in open court. The object is to avoid any suspicion that the clerk has been involved in deciding issues of fact.

The *Practice Direction* thus places a responsibility on those who advise magistrates in their judicial capacity to draw attention to any guidance relevant to the choice of penalty provided by the law and the decisions of the higher courts or other authorities. This includes the sentencing principles laid down by the Court of Appeal (above). A previous *Practice Direction* also indicated that it may be appropriate for the adviser to give information about sentences already imposed by the bench, or by neighbouring benches, in respect of similar offences to those being tried by the justices—since it is desirable to achieve uniformity of approach whenever possible.

Other considerations affecting judicial decision-making

Advice concerning judicial responsibilities in general would include, eg guidance on the rules of natural justice and correct approaches to decision-making, with an emphasis on the need to deal with cases on the basis only of relevant (ie legally relevant) considerations. To this might be added a duty to keep magistrates informed in a general sense about key developments affecting the performance of their duties— including any substantial legal changes—and about understandings or protocols with other agencies, as well eg as providing information about the local facilities and arrangements for community sentences. All these items affect the capacity of magistrates to make sound and appropriate judicial decisions and are an inescapable component of the judicial process.

In the retiring room

When magistrates adjourn to their private quarters to consider sentence it is good practice—whenever there are matters within the ambit of the *Practice Direction* and in all but the most straightforward cases—to consider seeking legal advice at some stage. In some instances this will need to be at the outset. However, the adviser should not retire with the magistrates as a matter of course (nor where the decision is a straightforward one which does not involve any legal or judicial considerations within the province of the adviser) and, if they do require advice, he or she should be audibly invited to join them.

If not sent for, the adviser is still entitled to go to the magistrates and to give them such advice as seems necessary—but he or she should inform the parties as to what is going to be said. Where the adviser has discussions with the justices *after* they have returned from retirement and the result is that they wish to retire again and on this occasion take the adviser with them, the parties should receive an explanation.

In practice, judicial advice is often given in open court and in the hearing of the parties—as envisaged by the *Practice Direction*. Where this is not the case, it is good practice for the parties to receive some explanation and, if appropriate, to be given the chance to make further representations before the court makes a final decision.

PERSONAL LIABILITY

Justices were warned by Lord Taylor, the late Lord Chief Justice, that if they fail to take appropriate advice on a settled legal point they could be held personally liable for the costs of any appeal. The case in question concerned an everyday matter, ie whether 'special reasons' for not endorsing a driving licence existed (*Chapter 7*) and salient advice—which was wrongly rejected—had been given both orally and in writing. This also emphasises the ever present need to be alert to the possibility that judicial advice may be essential in even the most run-of-the-mill cases.

FOREWORD

The National Mode of Trial Guidelines were produced in October 1990. They have proved extremely useful and helpful to magistrates having to decide whether or not to commit 'either way' offences to the Crown Court for trial. Now, they have been revised and brought up to date by the Secretariat of the Criminal Justice Consultative Council. The Secretariat and all those who have assisted them, from the Home Office, the Lord Chancellor's Department, the Law Officers Department, the Crown Prosecution Service, the Magistrates' Association and the Justices' Clerks are to be congratulated and thanked for their work.

It must be recognised that in this field as in others, guidelines are offered by way of assistance not as directions. That said, those who have the difficult decisions to make on Mode of Trial will find these revised guidelines most helpful. I commend them wholeheartedly.

Taylor CJ
Lord Chief Justice of England

NATIONAL MODE OF TRIAL GUIDELINES 1995

The purpose of these guidelines is to help magistrates decide whether or not to commit 'either way' offences for trial in the Crown Court. Their object is to provide guidance not direction. They are not intended to impinge upon a magistrate's duty to consider each case individually and on its own particular facts.

These guidelines apply to all defendants **aged 18 and above.**

General Mode of Trial Considerations
Section 19 of the Magistrates' Court Act 1980 requires magistrates to have regard to the following matters in deciding whether an offence is more suitable for summary trial or trial on indictment:

1. the nature of the case
2. whether the circumstances make the offence one of a serious character
3. whether the punishment which a magistrates' court would have power to inflict for it would be adequate

4. any other circumstances which appear to the court to make it more suitable for the offence to be tried in one way rather than the other
5. any representations made by the prosecution or the defence.

Certain general observations can be made:

a. the court should never make its decision on the grounds of convenience or expedition
b. the court should assume for the purpose of deciding mode of trial that the prosecution version of the facts is correct
c. the fact that the offences are alleged to be specimens is a relevant consideration; the fact that the defendant will be asking for other offences to be taken into consideration, if convicted, is not
d. where cases involve complex questions of fact or difficult questions of law, including difficult issues of disclosure of sensitive material, the court should consider committal for trial
e. where two or more defendants are jointly charged with an offence each has an individual right to elect his mode of trial. [This follows the decision in *R v Brentwood Justices ex parte Nicholls.*]
f. *in general, except where otherwise stated, either way offences should be tried summarily unless the court considers that the particular case has one or more of the features set out in the following pages and that its sentencing powers are insufficient.*
g. the court should also consider its power to commit an offender for sentence, under Section 38 of the Magistrates' Courts Act 1980, as amended by Section 25 of the Criminal Justice Act 1991, **if information emerges during the course of the hearing which leads them to conclude that the offence is so serious, or the offender such a risk to the public, that their powers to sentence him are inadequate.** This amendment means that committal for sentence is no longer determined by reference to the character or antecedents of the defendant.

Features Relevant to the Individual Offences

Note: Where reference is made in these guidelines to property or damage of 'high value' it means a figure equal to at least **twice** the amount of the limit (currently £5,000) imposed by statute on a magistrates' court when making a compensation order.

Burglary

> Cases should be tried summarily unless the court considers that one or more of the following features is present in the case and that its sentencing powers are insufficient.
> Magistrates should take account of their powers under S25 of the Criminal Justice Act 1991 to commit for **sentence.**
> *Note: See paragraph (g) on page [122].*

1. Dwelling House
1. Entry in the daytime when the occupier (or another) is present
2. Entry at night of a house which is normally occupied, whether or not the occupier (or another) is present
3. The offence is alleged to be one of a series of similar offences
4. When soiling, ransacking, damage or vandalism occurs
5. The offence has professional hallmarks
6. The unrecovered property is of high value (see [sbove] for definition of high value)

Note: Attention is drawn to para 28(c) of Schedule 1 of the Magistrates' Courts Act 1980, by which offences of burglary in a dwelling **cannot** be tried summarily if any person in the dwelling was subjected to violence or the threat of violence.

Burglary

> Cases should be tried summarily unless the court considers that one or more of the following features is present in the case and that its sentencing powers are insufficient.
> Magistrates should take account of their powers under S25 of the Criminal Justice Act 1991 to commit for **sentence.**
> *Note: See paragraph (g) on page [122].*

2. Non-Dwellings
1. Entry of a pharmacy or doctor's surgery
2. Fear is caused or violence is done to anyone lawfully on the premises (eg nightwatchman; security guard)
3. The offence has professional hallmarks
4. Vandalism on a substantial scale
5. The unrecovered property is of high value (see [above] for definition of high value)

Theft and Fraud

> Cases should be tried summarily unless the court considers that one or more of the following features is present in the case and that its sentencing powers are insufficient.
> Magistrates should take account of their powers under S25 of the Criminal Justice Act 1991 to commit for **sentence.**
> *Note: See paragraph (g) on page [122].*

1. Breach of trust by a person in a position of substantial authority, or in whom a high degree of trust is placed
2. Theft or fraud which has been committed or disguised in a sophisticated manner
3. Theft or fraud committed by an organised gang
4. The victim is particularly vulnerable to theft or fraud eg the elderly or infirm
5. The unrecovered property is of high value (see page [123] for definition of high value)

Handling

Cases should be tried summarily unless the court considers that one or more of the following features is present in the case and that its sentencing powers are insufficient.
   Magistrates should take account of their powers under S25 of the Criminal Justice Act 1991 to commit for **sentence**.
   Note: See paragraph (g) on page [122].

1. Dishonest handling of stolen property by a receiver who has commissioned the theft
2. The offence has professional hallmarks
3. The property is of high value (see page [123] for definition of high value)

Social Security Frauds

Cases should be tried summarily unless the court considers that one or more of the following features is present in the case and that its sentencing powers are insufficient.
   Magistrates should take account of their powers under S25 of the Criminal Justice Act 1991 to commit for **sentence**.
   Note: See paragraph (g) on page [122].

1. Organised fraud on a large scale
2. The frauds are substantial and carried out over a long period of time

Violence (Sections 20 and 47 of the Offences Against the Person Act 1861)

Cases should be tried summarily unless the court considers that one or more of the following features is present in the case and that its sentencing powers are insufficient.
   Magistrates should take account of their powers under S25 of the Criminal Justice Act 1991 to commit for **sentence**.
   Note: See paragraph (g) on page [122].

1. The use of a weapon of a kind likely to cause serious injury
2. A weapon is used and serious injury is caused
3. More than minor injury is caused by kicking, head butting or similar forms of assault
4. Serious violence is caused to those whose work has to be done in contact with the public or who are likely to face violence in the course of their work
5. Violence to vulnerable people eg the elderly or infirm
6. The offence has clear racial motivation

Note: The same considerations apply to cases of **domestic** violence.

Public Order Act Offences

Cases should be tried summarily unless the court considers that one or more of the following features is present in the case and that its sentencing powers are insufficient.

Magistrates should take account of their powers under S25 of the Criminal Justice Act 1991 to commit for **sentence.**

Note: See paragraph (g) on page [122].

1. Cases of **Violent Disorder** should generally be committed for trial
2. Affray
1. Organised violence or use of weapons
2. Significant injury or substantial damage
3. The offence has clear racial motivation
4. An attack upon police officers, prison officers, ambulance men, firemen and the like

Violence to and Neglect of Children

Cases should be tried summarily unless the court considers that one or more of the following features is present in the case and that its sentencing powers are insufficient.

Magistrates should take account of their powers under S25 of the Criminal Justice Act 1991 to commit for **sentence.**

Note: See paragraph (g) on page [122].

1. Substantial injury
2. Repeated violence or serious neglect, even if the physical harm is slight
3. Sadistic violence eg deliberate burning or scalding

Indecent Assault

Cases should be tried summarily unless the court considers that one or more of the following features is present in the case and that its sentencing powers are insufficient.

Magistrates should take account of their powers under S25 of the Criminal Justice Act 1991 to commit for **sentence.**

Note: See paragraph (g) on page [122].

1. Substantial disparity in age between victim and defendant, and the assault is more than trivial
2. Violence or threats of violence
3. Relationship of trust or responsibility between defendant and victim
4. Several similar offences, and the assaults are more than trivial
5. The victim is particularly vulnerable
6. Serious nature of the assault

Unlawful Sexual Intercourse

Cases should be tried summarily unless the court considers that one or more of the following features is present in the case and that its sentencing powers are insufficient.

Magistrates should take account of their powers under S25 of the Criminal Justice Act 1991 to commit for **sentence.**

Note: See paragraph (g) on page [122].

1. Wide disparity of age
2. Breach of position of trust
3. The victim is particularly vulnerable

Drugs

1. Class A

    a. Supply; possession with intent to supply.
       These cases should be committed for trial
    b. Possession
       Should be committed for trial unless the amount is
       consistent only with personal use

2. Class B

    a. Supply; possession with intent to supply.
       Should be committed for trial unless there is only small
       scale supply for no payment
    b. Possession
       Should be committed for trial when the quantity is
       substantial and not consistent only with personal use

Dangerous Driving

> Cases should be tried summarily unless the court considers that one or more of the following features is present in the case and that its sentencing powers are insufficient.
>   Magistrates should take account of their powers under S25 of the Criminal Justice Act 1991 to commit for **sentence.**
>   *Note: See paragraph (g) on page [122].*

1. Alcohol or drugs contributing to dangerousness
2. Grossly excessive speed
3. Racing
4. Prolonged course of dangerous driving
5. Degree of injury or damage sustained
6. Other related offences

Criminal Damage

> Cases should be tried summarily unless the court considers that one or more of the following features is present in the case and that its sentencing powers are insufficient.
>   Magistrates should take account of their powers under S25 of the Criminal Justice Act 1991 to commit for **sentence.**
>   *Note: See paragraph (g) on page [122].*

1. Deliberate fire-raising
2. Committed by group
3 Damage of a high value
4. The offence has clear racial motivation

Note: Offences set out in Schedule 2 of the Magistrates' Courts Act 1980 (which includes offences of criminal damage which do not amount to arson) must be tried summarily if the value of the property damaged or destroyed is £5,000 or less.

126

The plea before venue procedure introduced by section 49 Criminal Procedure and Investigations Act 1996 (see *Chapter 2*) requires a magistrates' court, when a defendant aged 18 or over *intimates* a guilty plea in relation to an *either way offence*, either:

- to proceed to sentence; or
- to commit to the Crown Court for sentence.

THE BASIC CONSIDERATION

Whether:

- on the basis of the information available to the magistrates' court
- the maximum sentencing powers available to magistrates of six months per offence (or possibly 12 months in aggregate if there are two or more either way offences) are sufficient in relation to the offence (or offences) in respect of which a guilty plea (or pleas) has (or have) been intimated.

This in turn requires the court to consider the seriousness of the offence or, if the offence is a violent or sexual offence and custody a prospect, the need to protect the public from serious harm from the offender: *Chapter 3*. On an intimation of guilty to an either way offence, courts should thus bear in mind:

- those indications of gravity contained in the *National Mode of Trial Guidelines*: see *Appendix A* to this handbook
- the *Magistrates' Association Sentencing Guidelines* (see *Appendix C*) or other, local sentencing guidelines
- whatever specific advice may be given about guidance from the higher courts: see the examples given in *Chapter 2, General Considerations* and *Chapter 11, Judicial Advice*
- the extent of any credit which ought to be allowed for an early guilty plea: *Chapter 1*.

GENERAL GUIDANCE

The general guidance set out in the following pages is based upon Court of Appeal rulings and should be borne in mind in relation to the particular offence listed:

Burglary: Dwelling

- Domestic burglary is, and always has been, regarded as a very serious offence. Sneak thefts (sometimes called 'walk-in' thefts) are the only burglaries of dwellings which may not merit consideration whether to commit to the Crown Court for sentence.

Burglary: Non Dwelling

- The *National Mode of Trial Guidelines* are highly relevant in deciding whether to send to the Crown Court for sentence.
- Any burglary of commercial premises where £1,000[1] or more is taken would normally indicate the need for the offender to be sentenced in the Crown Court.
- 'Ram-raiding' also indicates Crown Court.
- Where there is more than one charge (ie two or more non-dwelling burglaries) and it is clear that the offences have been committed whilst on bail, this would be another indication that the matter should be sent to the Crown Court for sentence.
- The court should always look at elements of planning and preparation, even if only a small amount has been taken.
- In respect of all types of burglary, the defendant's record is very relevant. Any suggestion that the defendant is a 'professional' indicates that the appropriate venue for sentence is the Crown Court.

Theft

- Systematic picking of pockets will normally indicate the Crown Court for sentence. This includes a defendant with one or two present offences who has a long record of such offences, including, eg thefts of purses or handbags.
- Thieves who steal from shops should go to the Crown Court where there is evidence of careful planning and the incident involves removal of goods of significant value.
- Thieves of livestock should be sent to the Crown Court for sentence. However, unlicensed fishers can be dealt with by magistrates when sentencing levels are well within magistrates' powers.
- Thieves who steal from phone boxes can normally be sentenced by magistrates unless there are indications of considerable difficulties caused by the prevalence of the offences.
- Thieves who steal lorries and cars for commercial gain should normally be sentenced at the Crown Court.

Theft in breach of trust
R v Barrick (1985) (7 Cr. App. R. (S.)) (as expanded on in *R v Clark, The Times,* 4 December 1997) is the guideline case concerning general considerations and parameters. The court should consider: (i) the amount involved; (ii) the period covered by the offence or offences; (ii) whether money taken was spent on necessities or luxuries; (iv) the effect on the victim; (v) the impact on public confidence; (vi) the effect on work colleagues; (vii) the effect on the offender; (viii) his or her own history; (ix) any help given to police.

Monetary threshold: Case law (and the *National Mode of Trial Guidelines*) indicate that magistrates' sentencing powers are not necessarily bound by a comparison with the upper compensation limit of £5,000 per offence and they may, if appropriate, sentence for offences where the value involved is up to £10,000. Where the victim is very vulnerable, eg an old person, some lesser amount may justify a committal to the Crown Court for sentence.

---

[1] This figure may be due for updating: 📖✍

Handling Stolen Goods

- If the goods involved are the proceeds of major crime, this will indicate that the matter should be sent to the Crown Court for sentence.
- Isolated handling by someone of good character can still be an indication that the matter should go to the Crown Court for sentence if the goods exceed £10,000 in value.*
- If the defendant is a 'regular' handler of proceeds of burglary, then this indicates that the Crown Court should sentence, especially where the court concludes that it is dealing with a 'professional' handler.

Abstracting Electricity

- Sentence will normally be within the magistrates' powers and accordingly these offences are unlikely to be sent to the Crown Court for sentence unless committed over a very long period and there is high value, ie £10,000 plus,* or where the evidence suggests commercial methods/organizations.

Making Off Without Paying

- Magistrates' sentencing powers would normally be sufficient.

'Going Equipped' for Theft, Burglary or Cheat

- Usually this offence can be sentenced summarily. However, if the items involved are obviously for a dwelling-house burglary (or some other serious offence such as large scale theft, or mortgage fraud) which would justify committal to the Crown Court for sentence in its own right, then committal for sentence may be appropriate.

Criminal Damage

a) Arson
- Magistrates should be reluctant to sentence in any case involving arson of a building. Damage must be minimal. Arson of other items may be sentenced by magistrates but they need to be satisfied that the fire could not have spread wider.

b) Other forms of damage
- Where the damage exceeds £10,000* and is clearly intentional (rather than reckless), then magistrates ought to consider sending the case to the Crown Court for sentence.
- Where the decision to commit for sentence may be finely balanced, any allegation of racist behaviour will be a pointer towards the matter being sent to the Crown Court for sentence.

Drugs

a) Cannabis

(i) Supply/possession with intent to supply

- The Court of Appeal has cast doubts on the usefulness of street value as a guide. If the defendant is a wholesaler and is dealing with 400 grammes or more then the matter should normally go to the Crown Court for sentence. At a lower level, where retailing is on a smaller scale, the matter should be sent to the Crown Court for sentence where the defendant is offering to supply in a general way rather than to a small group of friends. Where the evidence shows commercial supply (eg bags, wraps, scales, cash) this is generally an indication that the matter should go to the Crown Court for sentence. Sales to schoolchildren are another indication that the matter is serious and should go to the Crown Court.

(ii) Possession

- Normally magistrates' powers of sentencing are sufficient.

(iii) Cultivation

- If it is clear that cultivation is solely for personal use then magistrates' powers of sentencing are sufficient. However, if there is a substantial amount of drugs involved, committal to the Crown Court for sentence is justified.
- If cultivation is for commercial use then this should normally point towards the Crown Court for sentence.

b) *Heroin*

(i) Supply/possession with intent to supply

- Cases of this nature should normally go to the Crown Court for sentence. There have been many fatal overdoses and the Court of Appeal has said that the prevalence of an offence *is* capable of aggravating its seriousness.

(ii) Simple possession

- Where the drug is for the defendant's own use and there is a plea of guilty, the magistrates' sentencing powers may be sufficient.

c) *LSD*

(i) Supply/possession with intent to supply

- This should normally be committed to the Crown Court for sentence unless it is clear that a minimal amount was involved in the supply/intended supply, ie less than ten doses.

(ii) Possession

- The same comments as under *Heroin* above.

d) *Ecstasy (MDMA)*

(i) Supply/possession with intent to supply

- Unless the circumstances are exceptional, defendants should normally be sent to the Crown Court for sentence.

(ii) Possession

- If the drug is for the defendant's own use and there is a plea of guilty, the magistrates' sentencing powers may be sufficient.

e) *Amphetamine*

The same comments as under *Ecstasy* above.

Indecent Assault

- If the victim is a young girl the case ought to go to the Crown Court.
- Similarly, if the indecency is serious, eg touching the child with defendant's penis.
- Any suggestion of attempted penetration or use of force also indicates that the matter should be sent to the Crown Court for sentence; and digital interference with the vagina also indicates Crown Court for sentence.

- If there is any suggestion that the defendant is not of full adult capacity, the offence may be appropriate for sentence by magistrates.
- Where the victim is an adolescent girl who 'consents', consideration should still be given to sending the matter to the Crown Court for sentence where there are features such as digital interference or oral sex.
- Impulsive touching unaccompanied by threats may justify sentencing in the magistrates' court.

Unlawful Sexual Intercourse

The following factors may point to a committal for sentence:

- Wide disparity of age as between offender and victim.
- Breach of a position of trust.
- The victim being particularly vulnerable (eg young, old, infirm, mentally disadvantaged).

'Malicious Wounding': Grievous Bodily Harm (section 20)

- Offences under section 18 Offences Against the Person Act 1861 (wounding with *intent*) are *not* triable by magistrates. As a general rule, the closer a section 20 ('malicious wounding') offence is to a section 18 offence, then the stronger the case for committing the defendant to the Crown Court for sentence.
- Kicking to the head, especially if repeated, should lead to the conclusion that the matter be sent to the Crown Court for sentence. The same can be said of the use of a glass ('glassing'), where two year sentences of imprisonment are a regular feature of Court of Appeal decisions. It makes little difference whether the glass is held or thrown if it leads in either case to injury to the face.
- The use of a weapon likely to cause serious injury should again lead to the conclusion that the matter be sent to the Crown Court for sentence. Case law also suggests that head-butting, and the use of feet or teeth is considered as akin to the use of a weapon.

Violent Disorder

- The *National Mode of Trial Guidelines* recommend that magistrates should decline jurisdiction.
- Only in rare cases should intimation of a guilty plea lead magistrates to *sentence* for this offence. It would need to be low level disorder, bordering on affray, and a mild affray at that.
- The larger the group of people involved in the disorder, the more likely it is that committal for sentence should follow.

Possessing an Offensive Weapon

- Where the weapon is offensive *per se* (eg a flick knife) then a sentence in the region of three to six months imprisonment is within Court of Appeal guidelines and accordingly magistrates may wish to proceed to sentence.

---

* References to £10,000 result from a general and consistent application of the remarks contained in the paragraph *Monetary threshold* on page 128.

THE MAGISTRATES' ASSOCIATION

SENTENCING GUIDELINES

This edition of the Magistrates' Association Sentencing Guidelines has been produced in consultation with Stipendiary Magistrates and the Justices' Clerks' Society. Grateful thanks go to all those involved in this unique collaboration.

The Sentencing Guidelines are issued with the blessing of the Lord Chancellor and the Lord Chief Justice. The Guidelines are endorsed by the Justices' Clerks' Society.

Mrs A. R. Fuller
Chairman of Council

© The Magistrates' Association April 1997

'I think it most important that, within discretionary limits, magistrates' courts up and down the country should endeavour to approach sentencing with a measure of consistency, and I have no doubt that these guidelines will contribute powerfully to that end.'

The Rt. Hon. The Lord Bingham of Cornhill
Lord Chief Justice of England

Introduction and User Guide

1.   Introduction

The Magistrates' Association's *Sentencing Guidelines* cover offences with which magistrates deal regularly and frequently in the <u>adult criminal courts</u>. They provide a sentencing structure which sets out how to:

- establish the seriousness of each case
- determine the most appropriate way of dealing with it.

The *Sentencing Guidelines* provide a method for considering individual cases and a guideline from which discussion should properly flow; but <u>they are not a tariff and should never be used as such</u>.

2.   Using the sentencing structure

2.1   *General principles*

Only magistrates decide sentence.

The sentencing structure used was established by the Criminal Justice Act 1991. This re-affirmed the principle of *just deserts* so that any penalty must reflect the seriousness of the offence for which it is imposed and the personal circumstances of the offender. Magistrates must always start the sentencing process by taking full account of all the circumstances of the offence and making a judicial assessment of the seriousness category into which it falls.

In every case, the Criminal Justice Act 1991 requires you to consider:

- is discharge, compensation or a fine appropriate?
- is the offence serious enough for a community penalty?
- is it so serious that only custody is appropriate?

Only when the first assessment of seriousness has been made should offender related mitigation be taken into account. This may not be used to raise the first assessment of seriousness to a higher category; but it may lower it. For example, offender mitigation may bring the seriousness level below the custody threshold into the community sentence range.

MAGISTRATES' ASSOCIATION SENTENCING GUIDELINES

CONTENTS

2.2 Establishing the seriousness of the offence

The guidance for each offence is set for a case of average seriousness and the decision making process involves *establishing the seriousness of the case before the court compared with other offences of the same type.* Users should:

- consider the various seriousness indicators, remembering that some will carry more weight than others.

- make sure that all aggravating and mitigating factors are considered. The lists in the *Guidelines* are neither exhaustive nor a substitute for the personal judgement of magistrates. Factors which do not appear in the *Guidelines* may be important in individual cases.

- always bear in mind that the commission of an offence on bail aggravates its seriousness.

- take care in using previous convictions or any failure to respond to previous sentences in assessing seriousness. We recommend that courts should identify any convictions relevant for this purpose and then consider to what extent they affect the seriousness of the present offence.

- note that when there are several offences before the court, the totality principle requires a court to consider the total sentence in relation to the totality of the offending and in relation to sentence levels for other crimes.

When you have formed an initial assessment of the seriousness of the offence, consider the offender.

2.3 Using offender mitigation

The guidelines set out some examples of offender mitigation but there are frequently others to be considered in individual cases. Any offender mitigation which the court accepts must lead to some downward revision of the initial assessment of seriousness, although this revision may sometimes be very minor.

A previous criminal record may reduce offender mitigation.

2.4 Sentence discount

The law requires that the court reduces the sentence for a timely guilty plea but this provision should be used with judicial flexibility. A timely guilty plea may attract a sentencing discount of up to one third but the precise amount of discount will depend on the facts of each case and a last minute plea of guilty may attract only a minimal reduction.

Discount may be given in respect of the fine or periods of community service or custody. Periods of mandatory disqualification or mandatory penalty points cannot be reduced for a guilty plea.

2.5 The available penalties

2.5.1 Absolute discharge

This should be used in the most minor of cases. It acknowledges that an offence has been committed but marks the court's intention to take no further action.

2.5.2 Conditional discharge

This is a useful disposal in minor cases where the court needs a sanction which directly discourages further offending.

2.5.3 Compensation

Magistrates have the power to award compensation for personal injury, loss or damage up to a total of £5,000 for each offence, including offences taken into consideration; and have a duty always to consider compensation in appropriate cases. When pronouncing sentence you must give an explanation in open court if you decide not to make an award.

Nevertheless, magistrates should not become involved in disputed and complicated cases. Compensation should only be awarded in clear, uncomplicated cases, and the following points need to be borne in mind.

- personal injury need not mean physical injury, eg. an award may be made for terror or distress resulting from an offence.

- compensation may not generally be awarded for injury, loss or damage resulting from a road accident. Consult your clerk for advice in any cases where this point arises.

- where compensation is awarded for damage, the cost of any necessary repairs must be proved to the satisfaction of the court.

In fixing the amount of a compensation order, the defendant's means must be taken into account and the order should normally be payable within twelve months. In exceptional circumstances it may be payable within a period of up to three years; but courts should always consider whether such an extended order is in the interests of the victim.

A table of suggested awards is set out on page viii.

- probation orders, with or without special requirements (six months to three years)

- community service orders (40-240 hours unpaid work)

- combination orders (1-3 years probation plus 40-100 hours of community service)

It is good practice always to order a pre-sentence report when a community penalty is under consideration.

The restrictions on liberty imposed by the sentence must be commensurate with the seriousness of the offence and the order must be the one most suitable for the offender. Rehabilitation is a factor to be taken into account in sentencing and a community penalty may be particularly appropriate for this purpose.

2.5.6   Custody

Custody is only appropriate where the offence is so serious that no other form of disposal is justified. It is good practice to order a pre-sentence report before imposing custody.

An offence is so serious that only custody is appropriate when right thinking members of the public, knowing all the facts, would feel that justice had not been done by the passing of any sentence other than a custodial one. R v Cox (1993) 96 Cr. App. R. 452.455.

3.   The role of the justices' clerk/court clerk in sentencing

Sentencing is a complex field. Although the decision on sentence rests entirely with the bench, the clerk is under a duty to advise on available sentences and on any case law that may apply to particular types of offence. It is especially important to ask for advice when the bench is considering imposing a custodial sentence.

The clerk's role is described by a Practice Direction issued by the Lord Chief Justice in 1981:

If it appears to him necessary to do so, or he is requested by the justices, the justices' clerk has the responsibility to ... advise the justices generally on the range of penalties which the law allows them to impose and on any guidance relevant to the decisions of the superior courts and other authorities.

2.5.4   Fines

Fines are appropriate for cases which are neither serious enough to attract a community penalty nor so serious that only custody is appropriate. The level of fine for any offence must be commensurate with the seriousness of the offence and must take the offender's means into account

The fine must not exceed the upper limit set by statute for the level of the offence. ie.

For a level 1 offence: £200
For a level 2 offence: £500
For a level 3 offence: £1,000
For a level 4 offence: £2,500
For a level 5 offence: £5,000

Before fixing the amount of the fine, the court must enquire into the offender's financial circumstances and we recommend the regular use of means forms.

The Guideline fines in this publication are set at three levels:

Low income   - about £100 net per week from all sources
Average income - about £250 net per week from all sources
High income   - about £600 net per week from all sources

The fines have not been discounted for a guilty plea.

The principle behind determining the amount of a fine should be that of equality of hardship rather than equality of monetary penalty. Punishment does not lie in the amount of a fine but in the degree of hardship and inconvenience caused by the need to pay it. The just deserts principle means that each offender should experience the loss of spending power which his or her offending behaviour merits, and levels of fine should always be set with this principle in mind.

Fines are due to be paid at the time they are imposed. Where time to pay is allowed it should not exceed twelve months: in these circumstances best practice should be to order an amount to be paid immediately and then to set a realistic weekly amount, and a date for a court hearing for compliance with the order to be reviewed.

2.5.5   Community penalties

Where the offence is serious enough a community penalty will be used. They are:

- attendance centre orders (12-36 hours)

Compensation Orders

Priorities

Compensation is an order in its own right, and should be treated as such - particularly where the offender has insufficient means to pay a fine as well.

Damages

Where compensation is to be awarded for damage to, for example, a window, the cost must be proved or agreed.

Payment by instalments

An order for compensation should normally be payable within 12 months, but this can be exceeded up to a three year limit where the circumstances justify it.

Giving reasons

Section 35, Powers of the Criminal Courts Act 1973 states that

'A court shall give reasons on passing sentence if it does not make (a compensation) order in a case where this section empowers it to do so'.

Powers and limitations

Magistrates have power to award compensation for personal injury loss or damage up to a total of £5,000 for each offence. The compensation may relate to offences taken into consideration. There are exceptions including injury, loss or damage due to a road accident unless the damage results from an offence under the Theft Act 1968 or the offender is uninsured and the Motor Insurers Bureau will not cover the loss - if in any doubt, seek advice from the clerk.

An order for compensation should be considered whether or not there is an application by or on behalf of the victim. An award in the magistrates' court will not preclude a civil claim. 'Personal injury' need not be a physical injury. An award can be made, eg, for terror or distress caused by the offence.

Criminal Injuries Compensation Board

The Criminal Injuries Compensation Scheme is intended to compensate victims of violent crime and particularly those who are seriously injured. The minimum award is currently £1,000. Courts are encouraged to order offenders to compensate the victim whether or not the injury comes within the scope of the Criminal Injuries Compensation Scheme, in order to bring home to offenders the personal consequences of their actions. To prevent double compensation for the same injury the Scheme provides for an award to be reduced by the amount of any compensation previously ordered by a criminal court.

Suggested compensation

Damages are assessed under two main headings – **general damages**, which is compensation for the pain and suffering of the injury itself and for any loss of facility; and **special damages**, which is compensation for financial loss sustained as a result of the injury - eg, loss of earnings, dental expenses etc. The suggestions given in the table on the following page are for general damages.

The following guidelines are taken from the Home Office Circular issued in August 1993.

The figures below are only a very general guide and may be increased or decreased according to the medical evidence, the victim's sex, age and any other factors which appear to the court to be relevant in the particular case. If the court does not have enough information to make a decision, then the matter should be adjourned to obtain more facts.

TYPE OF INJURY		SUGGESTED AWARD
Graze	depending on size	up to £50
Bruise	depending on size	up to £75
Black eye		£100
Cut: no permanent scarring	depending on size and whether stitched	£75-£500
Sprain	depending on loss of mobility	£100-£1,000
Loss of a non-front tooth	depending on cosmetic effect and age of victim	£250-£500
Other minor injury	causing reasonable absence from work (2-3) weeks	£550-£850
Loss of a front tooth		£1,000
Facial scar	however small - resulting in permanent disfigurement	£750+
Jaw	fractured (wired)	£2,750
Nasal	undisplaced fracture of the nasal bone	£750
Nasal	displaced fracture of bone requiring manipulation	£1,000
Nasal	not causing fracture but displaced septum requiring sub-mucous resection	£1,750
Wrist	simple fracture with complete recovery in a few weeks	£1,750-£2,500
Wrist	displaced fracture - limb in plaster for some 6 weeks; full recovery 6-12 months	£2,500+
Finger	fractured little finger; assuming full recovery after a few weeks	£750
Leg or arm	simple fracture of tibia, fibula, ulna or radius with full recovery in three weeks	£2,500
Laparotomy	stomach scar 6-8 inches long (resulting from exploratory operation)	£3,500

Aggravated Vehicle-taking

Theft Act 1968 s. 12A as inserted by
Aggravated Vehicle-Taking Act 1992
Triable either way - but in certain cases
summarily only - consult clerk.
Penalty: Level 5 and/or 6 months
Must endorse and disqualify at least 12 months.

CONSIDER THE SERIOUSNESS OF THE OFFENCE
(INCLUDING THE IMPACT ON THE VICTIM)

IS COMPENSATION, DISCHARGE OR FINE APPROPRIATE?
IS IT SERIOUS ENOUGH FOR A COMMUNITY PENALTY?

GUIDELINE: >—   IS IT SO SERIOUS THAT ONLY CUSTODY IS APPROPRIATE?
ARE MAGISTRATES' COURTS' POWERS APPROPRIATE?

 CONSIDER AGGRAVATING AND MITIGATING FACTORS

for example
- Avoiding detection or apprehension
- Competitive driving: racing, showing off
- Disregard of warnings eg from passengers
  or others in vicinity
- Group action
- Pre-mediated
- Serious injury/damage
- Serious risk

for example
- Impulsive
- No competitiveness/racing
- Passenger only
- Single incident of bad driving
- Speed not excessive
- Very minor injury/damage
- This list is not exhaustive

- Offence committed on bail
- Previous convictions and failures to respond
  to previous sentences, if relevant
- This list is not exhaustive

CONSIDER OFFENDER MITIGATION

for example
- Age, health (physical or mental)
- Co-operation with the police
- Voluntary compensation
- Remorse

CONSIDER YOUR SENTENCE

*Compare it with the suggested guideline level of sentence and reconsider
your reasons carefully if you have chosen a sentence at a different level.
Consider a discount for a timely guilty plea.*

DECIDE YOUR SENTENCE

NB. COMPENSATION - Give reasons if not awarding compensation

Remember: These are GUIDELINES not a tariff

Affray

Public Order Act 1986 s.3
Triable either way - see Mode of Trial Guidelines
Penalty: Level 5 and/or 6 months

CONSIDER THE SERIOUSNESS OF THE OFFENCE
(INCLUDING THE IMPACT ON THE VICTIM)

IS COMPENSATION, DISCHARGE OR FINE APPROPRIATE?
IS IT SERIOUS ENOUGH FOR A COMMUNITY PENALTY?

GUIDELINE: >—   IS IT SO SERIOUS THAT ONLY CUSTODY IS APPROPRIATE?
ARE MAGISTRATES' COURTS' POWERS APPROPRIATE?

 CONSIDER AGGRAVATING AND MITIGATING FACTORS

for example
- Racial motivation
- Busy public place
- Group action
- People actually put in fear
- Vulnerable victim(s)

for example
- Offender acting alone
- Provocation
- Did not start the trouble
- Stopped as soon as the police arrived
- This list is not exhaustive

- Offence committed on bail
- Previous convictions and failures to respond
  to previous sentences, if relevant
- This list is not exhaustive

CONSIDER OFFENDER MITIGATION

for example
- Age, health (physical or mental)
- Co-operation with the police
- Voluntary compensation
- Remorse

CONSIDER YOUR SENTENCE

*Compare it with the suggested guideline level of sentence and reconsider
your reasons carefully if you have chosen a sentence at a different level.
Consider a discount for a timely guilty plea.*

DECIDE YOUR SENTENCE

NB. COMPENSATION - Give reasons if not awarding compensation

Remember: These are GUIDELINES not a tariff

Assault on a Police Officer

Police Act 1996 s.89
Triable only summarily
Penalty: Level 5 and/or 6 months

CONSIDER THE SERIOUSNESS OF THE OFFENCE
(INCLUDING THE IMPACT ON THE VICTIM)

IS COMPENSATION, DISCHARGE OR FINE APPROPRIATE?
IS IT SERIOUS ENOUGH FOR A COMMUNITY PENALTY?

GUIDELINE: ➤ *IS IT SO SERIOUS THAT ONLY CUSTODY IS APPROPRIATE?*

➕ CONSIDER AGGRAVATING AND MITIGATING FACTORS ➖

for example
Any injuries caused
Gross disregard for police authority
Group action
Premeditated

Offence committed on bail
Previous convictions and failures to respond
to previous sentences, if relevant
This list is not exhaustive

for example
Impulsive action
Unaware that person was a Police Officer
This list is not exhaustive

CONSIDER OFFENDER MITIGATION

for example
Age, health (physical or mental)
Co-operation with the police
Voluntary compensation
Remorse

CONSIDER YOUR SENTENCE

Compare it with the suggested guideline level of sentence and reconsider
your reasons carefully if you have chosen a sentence at a different level.
Consider a discount for a timely guilty plea.

DECIDE YOUR SENTENCE

NB. COMPENSATION - Give reasons if not awarding compensation

Remember: These are GUIDELINES not a tariff

Offences Against the Person Act 1861 s.47
Triable either way - **see Mode of Trial Guidelines**
Penalty: Level 5 and/or 6 months

Assault —
Actual Bodily Harm

CONSIDER THE SERIOUSNESS OF THE OFFENCE
(INCLUDING THE IMPACT ON THE VICTIM)

IS COMPENSATION, DISCHARGE OR FINE APPROPRIATE?
IS IT SERIOUS ENOUGH FOR A COMMUNITY PENALTY?
IS IT SO SERIOUS THAT ONLY CUSTODY IS APPROPRIATE?

GUIDELINE: ➤ *ARE MAGISTRATES' COURTS' POWERS APPROPRIATE?*

➕ CONSIDER AGGRAVATING AND MITIGATING FACTORS ➖

for example
Racial motivation
Deliberate kicking or biting
Extensive injuries (may be psychiatric)
Group action
Offender in position of authority
Premeditated
Victim particularly vulnerable
Victim serving public
Weapon

Offence committed on bail
Previous convictions and failures to respond
to previous sentences, if relevant
This list is not exhaustive

for example
Impulsive
Minor injury
Provocation
Single blow
This list is not exhaustive

CONSIDER OFFENDER MITIGATION

for example
Age, health (physical or mental)
Co-operation with the police
Voluntary compensation
Remorse

CONSIDER YOUR SENTENCE

Compare it with the suggested guideline level of sentence and reconsider
your reasons carefully if you have chosen a sentence at a different level.
Consider a discount for a timely guilty plea.

DECIDE YOUR SENTENCE

NB. COMPENSATION - Give reasons if not awarding compensation

Remember: These are GUIDELINES not a tariff

Burglary (Dwelling)

Theft Act 1968 s.9
Triable either way - see Mode of Trial Guidelines
Penalty: Level 5 and/or 6 months

CONSIDER THE SERIOUSNESS OF THE OFFENCE
(INCLUDING THE IMPACT ON THE VICTIM)

GUIDELINE: >
IS COMPENSATION, DISCHARGE OR FINE APPROPRIATE?
IS IT SERIOUS ENOUGH FOR A COMMUNITY PENALTY?
IS IT SO SERIOUS THAT ONLY CUSTODY IS APPROPRIATE?
ARE MAGISTRATES' COURTS' POWERS APPROPRIATE?

– CONSIDER AGGRAVATING AND MITIGATING FACTORS

for example
Racial motivation
Deliberately frightening occupants
Group offence
People in house
Professional operation
Forcible entry
Soiling, ransacking, damage

Offence committed on bail
Previous convictions and failures to respond
to previous sentences, if relevant
This list is not exhaustive

for example
Low value
Nobody frightened
No damage or disturbance
No forcible entry
Opportunist
This list is not exhaustive

CONSIDER OFFENDER MITIGATION

for example
Age, health (physical or mental)
Co-operation with the police
Voluntary compensation
Remorse

CONSIDER YOUR SENTENCE

Compare it with the suggested guideline level of sentence and reconsider
your reasons carefully if you have chosen a sentence at a different level.
Consider a discount for a timely guilty plea.

DECIDE YOUR SENTENCE

NB. COMPENSATION - Give reasons if not awarding compensation

Remember: These are GUIDELINES not a tariff

Burglary (Non-dwelling)

Theft Act 1968 s.9
Triable either way - see Mode of Trial Guidelines
Penalty: Level 5 and/or 6 months

CONSIDER THE SERIOUSNESS OF THE OFFENCE
(INCLUDING THE IMPACT ON THE VICTIM)

GUIDELINE: >
IS COMPENSATION, DISCHARGE OR FINE APPROPRIATE?
IS IT SERIOUS ENOUGH FOR A COMMUNITY PENALTY?
IS IT SO SERIOUS THAT ONLY CUSTODY IS APPROPRIATE?
ARE MAGISTRATES' COURTS' POWERS APPROPRIATE?

– CONSIDER AGGRAVATING AND MITIGATING FACTORS

for example
Racial motivation
Deliberately frightening occupants
Group offence
Night time
Professional operation
Forcible entry
Soiling, ransacking, damage
Serious harm to business

Offence committed on bail
Previous convictions and failures to respond
to previous sentences, if relevant
This list is not exhaustive

for example
Low value
Nobody frightened
No damage or disturbance
No forcible entry
This list is not exhaustive

CONSIDER OFFENDER MITIGATION

for example
Age, health (physical or mental)
Co-operation with the police
Voluntary compensation
Remorse

CONSIDER YOUR SENTENCE

Compare it with the suggested guideline level of sentence and reconsider
your reasons carefully if you have chosen a sentence at a different level.
Consider a discount for a timely guilty plea.

DECIDE YOUR SENTENCE

NB. COMPENSATION - Give reasons if not awarding compensation

Remember: These are GUIDELINES not a tariff

Misuse of Drugs Act 1971
Triable either way - see Mode of Trial Guidelines
Penalty: Level 5 and/or 6 months

Class A Drugs – Possession

CONSIDER THE SERIOUSNESS OF THE OFFENCE

IS COMPENSATION, DISCHARGE OR FINE APPROPRIATE?

IS IT SERIOUS ENOUGH FOR A COMMUNITY PENALTY?

GUIDELINE: > IS IT SO SERIOUS THAT ONLY CUSTODY IS APPROPRIATE?

ARE MAGISTRATES' COURTS' POWERS APPROPRIATE?

 CONSIDER AGGRAVATING AND MITIGATING FACTORS —

for example

An amount other than a very small quantity

Offence committed on bail
Previous convictions and failures to respond
to previous sentences, if relevant
This list is not exhaustive

for example
Very small quantity
This list is not exhaustive

CONSIDER OFFENDER MITIGATION

for example
Age, health (physical or mental)
Co-operation with the police
Remorse

CONSIDER YOUR SENTENCE

*Compare it with the suggested guideline level of sentence and reconsider
your reasons carefully if you have chosen a sentence at a different level.
Consider a discount for a timely guilty plea. Consider forfeiture and destruction.*

DECIDE YOUR SENTENCE

Remember: These are GUIDELINES not a tariff

Misuse of Drugs Act 1971
Triable either way - see Mode of Trial Guidelines
Penalty: Level 5 and/or 6 months

Class A Drugs – Production, Supply

CONSIDER THE SERIOUSNESS OF THE OFFENCE
(INCLUDING THE IMPACT ON THE VICTIM)

IS COMPENSATION, DISCHARGE OR FINE APPROPRIATE?

IS IT SERIOUS ENOUGH FOR A COMMUNITY PENALTY?

GUIDELINE: > IS IT SO SERIOUS THAT ONLY CUSTODY IS APPROPRIATE?

ARE MAGISTRATES' COURTS' POWERS APPROPRIATE?

+ **CONSIDER AGGRAVATING AND MITIGATING FACTORS** —

for example

Commercial production
Large amount
Deliberate adulteration
Venue, eg. prisons, educational
establishments
Sophisticated operation

Offence committed on bail
Previous convictions and failures to respond
to previous sentences, if relevant
This list is not exhaustive

for example
Small amount
This list is not exhaustive

CONSIDER OFFENDER MITIGATION

for example
Age, health (physical or mental)
Co-operation with the police
Remorse

CONSIDER YOUR SENTENCE

*Compare it with the suggested guideline level of sentence and reconsider
your reasons carefully if you have chosen a sentence at a different level.
Consider a discount for a timely guilty plea. Consider forfeiture and destruction.*

DECIDE YOUR SENTENCE

Remember: These are GUIDELINES not a tariff

Misuse of Drugs Act 1971
Triable either way - see Mode of Trial Guidelines
Penalty: Level 5 and/or 6 months

Class B Drugs — Supply:
Possession with intent to supply

CONSIDER THE SERIOUSNESS OF THE OFFENCE
(INCLUDING THE IMPACT ON THE VICTIM)

GUIDELINE: ➢ IS COMPENSATION, DISCHARGE OR FINE APPROPRIATE?
IS IT SERIOUS ENOUGH FOR A COMMUNITY PENALTY?
IS IT SO SERIOUS THAT ONLY CUSTODY IS APPROPRIATE?
ARE MAGISTRATES' COURTS' POWERS APPROPRIATE?

+ CONSIDER AGGRAVATING AND MITIGATING FACTORS −

for example	for example
Commercial production	Not commercial
Large amount	Small amount
Venue, eg. prisons, educational	*This list is not exhaustive*
establishments	
Deliberate adulteration	
Offence committed on bail	
Previous convictions and failures to respond	
to previous sentences, if relevant	
This list is not exhaustive	

CONSIDER OFFENDER MITIGATION

for example
Age, health (physical or mental)
Co-operation with the police
Remorse

CONSIDER YOUR SENTENCE

*Compare it with the suggested guideline level of sentence and reconsider
your reasons carefully. If you have chosen a sentence at a different level.
Consider a discount for a timely guilty plea. Consider forfeiture and destruction.*

DECIDE YOUR SENTENCE

Remember: These are GUIDELINES not a tariff

Misuse of Drugs Acts 1971
Triable either way - see Mode of Trial Guidelines
Penalty: Level 4 and/or 3 months

Class B Drugs —
Possession

CONSIDER THE SERIOUSNESS OF THE OFFENCE

GUIDELINE: ➢ IS COMPENSATION, DISCHARGE OR FINE APPROPRIATE?
IS IT SERIOUS ENOUGH FOR A COMMUNITY PENALTY?
IS IT SO SERIOUS THAT ONLY CUSTODY IS APPROPRIATE?
ARE MAGISTRATES' COURTS' POWERS APPROPRIATE?

+ CONSIDER AGGRAVATING AND MITIGATING FACTORS −

for example	for example
Large amount	Small amount
	This list is not exhaustive
Offence committed on bail	
Previous convictions and failures to respond	
to previous sentences, if relevant	
This list is not exhaustive	

CONSIDER OFFENDER MITIGATION

for example
Age, health (physical or mental)
Co-operation with the police
Remorse

CONSIDER YOUR SENTENCE

*Compare it with the suggested guideline level of sentence and reconsider
your reasons carefully. If you have chosen a sentence at a different level.
Consider a discount for a timely guilty plea. Consider forfeiture and destruction.*

DECIDE YOUR SENTENCE

GUIDELINE FINES		
LOW INCOME	AVERAGE INCOME	HIGH INCOME
£90	£225	£540

Remember: These are GUIDELINES not a tariff

Criminal Damage

Criminal Damage Act 1971 s.1
Triable either way or summarily only. Consult Clerk
Penalty: Either way - Level 5 and/or 6 months
Summarily - Level 4 and/or 3 months

CONSIDER THE SERIOUSNESS OF THE OFFENCE
(INCLUDING THE IMPACT ON THE VICTIM)

GUIDELINE: ➤ IS COMPENSATION, DISCHARGE OR FINE APPROPRIATE?
IS IT SERIOUS ENOUGH FOR A COMMUNITY PENALTY?
IS IT SO SERIOUS THAT ONLY CUSTODY IS APPROPRIATE?
ARE MAGISTRATES' COURTS' POWERS APPROPRIATE?

⊕ CONSIDER AGGRAVATING AND MITIGATING FACTORS ⊖

for example
Racial motivation
Deliberate
Group offence
Serious damage

Offence committed on bail
Previous convictions and failures to respond
to previous sentences, if relevant
This list is not exhaustive

for example
Impulsive action
Minor damage
Provocation
This list is not exhaustive

CONSIDER OFFENDER MITIGATION

for example
Age, health (physical or mental)
Co-operation with the police
Voluntary compensation
Remorse

CONSIDER YOUR SENTENCE

*Compare it with the suggested guideline level of sentence and reconsider
your reasons carefully if you have chosen a sentence at a different level.
Consider a discount for a timely guilty plea.*

DECIDE YOUR SENTENCE

GUIDELINE FINES		
LOW INCOME	AVERAGE INCOME	HIGH INCOME
£135	£340	£810

NB. COMPENSATION - Give reasons if not awarding compensation

Remember: These are GUIDELINES not a tariff

© The Magistrates' Association   12   Issue April 1997

Common Assault

Criminal Justice Act 1988 s.39
Triable only summarily
Penalty: Level 5 and/or 6 months

CONSIDER THE SERIOUSNESS OF THE OFFENCE
(INCLUDING THE IMPACT ON THE VICTIM)

GUIDELINE: ➤ IS COMPENSATION, DISCHARGE OR FINE APPROPRIATE?
IS IT SERIOUS ENOUGH FOR A COMMUNITY PENALTY?
IS IT SO SERIOUS THAT ONLY CUSTODY IS APPROPRIATE?

⊕ CONSIDER AGGRAVATING AND MITIGATING FACTORS ⊖

for example
Racial motivation
Group action
Offender in position of authority
Premeditated
Injury
Weapon
Victim particularly vulnerable
Victim public servant

Offence committed on bail
Previous convictions and failures to respond
to previous sentences, if relevant
This list is not exhaustive

for example
Impulsive
Minor injury
Provocation
Single blow
This list is not exhaustive

CONSIDER OFFENDER MITIGATION

for example
Age, health (physical or mental)
Co-operation with the police
Voluntary compensation
Remorse

CONSIDER YOUR SENTENCE

*Compare it with the suggested guideline level of sentence and reconsider
your reasons carefully if you have chosen a sentence at a different level.
Consider a discount for a timely guilty plea.*

DECIDE YOUR SENTENCE

NB. COMPENSATION - Give reasons if not awarding compensation

Remember: These are GUIDELINES not a tariff

© The Magistrates' Association   11   Issue April 1997

Misuse of Drugs Act 1971
Triable either way - see Mode of Trial Guideline
Penalty: Level 5 and/or 6 months

Cultivation of Cannabis

CONSIDER THE SERIOUSNESS OF THE OFFENCE

GUIDELINE: ➤ IS COMPENSATION, DISCHARGE OR FINE APPROPRIATE?
IS IT SERIOUS ENOUGH FOR A COMMUNITY PENALTY?
IS IT SO SERIOUS THAT ONLY CUSTODY IS APPROPRIATE?
ARE MAGISTRATES' COURTS' POWERS APPROPRIATE?

 CONSIDER AGGRAVATING AND MITIGATING FACTORS

for example
Commercial cultivation
Large quantity

Offence committed on bail
Previous convictions and failures to respond
to previous sentences, if relevant
This list is not exhaustive

for example
For personal use
Not commercial
Not responsible for planting
Small scale cultivation
This list is not exhaustive

CONSIDER OFFENDER MITIGATION

for example
Age, health (physical or mental)
Co-operation with the police
Remorse

CONSIDER YOUR SENTENCE

Compare it with the suggested guideline level of sentence and reconsider
your reasons carefully if you have chosen a sentence at a different level.
Consider a discount for a timely guilty plea. Consider forfeiture and destruction.

DECIDE YOUR SENTENCE

GUIDELINE FINES		
LOW INCOME	AVERAGE INCOME	HIGH INCOME
£90	£225	£540

Remember: These are GUIDELINES not a tariff

 Issue April 1997

Drunk and Disorderly

CONSIDER THE SERIOUSNESS OF THE OFFENCE

GUIDELINE: ➤ IS COMPENSATION, DISCHARGE OR FINE APPROPRIATE?
IS IT SERIOUS ENOUGH FOR A COMMUNITY PENALTY?
(PROBATION IS ONLY AVAILABLE COMMUNITY PENALTY FOR THIS OFFENCE)

 CONSIDER AGGRAVATING AND MITIGATING FACTORS

for example
Offensive language or behaviour
With group

Offence committed on bail
Previous convictions and failures to respond
to previous sentences, if relevant
This list is not exhaustive

for example
Induced by others
No significant disturbance
Not threatening
This list is not exhaustive

CONSIDER OFFENDER MITIGATION

for example
Age, health (physical or mental)
Co-operation with the police
Remorse

CONSIDER YOUR SENTENCE

Compare it with the suggested guideline level of sentence and reconsider
your reasons carefully if you have chosen a sentence at a different level.
Consider a discount for a timely guilty plea.

DECIDE YOUR SENTENCE

GUIDELINE FINES		
LOW INCOME	AVERAGE INCOME	HIGH INCOME
£45	£115	£270

Remember: These are GUIDELINES not a tariff

 Issue April 1997

Theft Act 1968 s.25
Triable either way - see Mode of Trial Guidelines
Penalty: Level 5 and/or 6 months
May disqualify where committed with reference to the theft
or taking of the vehicle

Going Equipped for Theft etc.

CONSIDER THE SERIOUSNESS OF THE OFFENCE

GUIDELINE: >
IS COMPENSATION, DISCHARGE OR FINE APPROPRIATE?
IS IT SERIOUS ENOUGH FOR A COMMUNITY PENALTY?
IS IT SO SERIOUS THAT ONLY CUSTODY IS APPROPRIATE?
ARE MAGISTRATES' COURTS' POWERS APPROPRIATE?

 ## CONSIDER AGGRAVATING AND MITIGATING FACTORS

for example
Premeditated
Group action
Sophisticated
Specialised equipment
Number of items
People put in fear

Offence committed on bail
Previous convictions and failures to respond
to previous sentences, if relevant
This list is not exhaustive

CONSIDER OFFENDER MITIGATION

for example
Age, health (physical or mental)
Co-operation with the police
Remorse

CONSIDER YOUR SENTENCE

Compare it with the suggested guideline level of sentence and reconsider
your reasons carefully if you have chosen a sentence at a different level.
Consider a discount for a timely guilty plea. Consider forfeiture.

DECIDE YOUR SENTENCE

Remember: These are GUIDELINES not a tariff

Bail Act 1976 s.6
Triable only summarily
Penalty: Level 5 and/or 3 months

Failure to Surrender to Bail

CONSIDER THE SERIOUSNESS OF THE OFFENCE

GUIDELINE: >
IS COMPENSATION, DISCHARGE OR FINE APPROPRIATE?
IS IT SERIOUS ENOUGH FOR A COMMUNITY PENALTY?
IS IT SO SERIOUS THAT ONLY CUSTODY IS APPROPRIATE?

 ## CONSIDER AGGRAVATING AND MITIGATING FACTORS

for example
Leaves jurisdiction
Wilful evasion
Appears after arrest

Offence committed on bail
Previous convictions and failures to respond
to previous sentences, if relevant
This list is not exhaustive

for example
Appears late on day of hearing
Genuine misunderstanding
Voluntary surrender
This list is not exhaustive

CONSIDER OFFENDER MITIGATION

for example
Age, health (physical or mental)
Co-operation with the police
Remorse

CONSIDER YOUR SENTENCE

Compare it with the suggested guideline level of sentence and reconsider
your reasons carefully if you have chosen a sentence at a different level.
Consider a discount for a timely guilty plea.

DECIDE YOUR SENTENCE

GUIDELINE FINES		
LOW INCOME	AVERAGE INCOME	HIGH INCOME
£60	£150	£350

Remember: These are GUIDELINES not a tariff

Harassment, Alarm or Distress

Public Order Act 1986 s.5
Triable only summarily
Penalty: Level 3

CONSIDER THE SERIOUSNESS OF THE OFFENCE
(INCLUDING THE IMPACT ON THE VICTIM)

GUIDELINE: ➤   *IS COMPENSATION, DISCHARGE OR FINE APPROPRIATE?*
     IS IT SERIOUS ENOUGH FOR A COMMUNITY PENALTY?
     (PROBATION IS ONLY AVAILABLE COMMUNITY PENALTY FOR THIS OFFENCE)

 CONSIDER AGGRAVATING AND MITIGATING FACTORS ⊖

for example
- Racial motivation
- Group action
- Vulnerable victim

- Offence committed on bail
- Previous convictions and failures to respond
  to previous sentences, if relevant
- *This list is not exhaustive*

for example
- Stopped as soon as police arrived
- Trivial incident
- *This list is not exhaustive*

CONSIDER OFFENDER MITIGATION

for example
- Age, health (physical or mental)
- Co-operation with the police
- Voluntary compensation
- Remorse

CONSIDER YOUR SENTENCE

*Compare it with the suggested guideline level of sentence and reconsider
your reasons carefully if you have chosen a sentence at a different level.
Consider a discount for a timely guilty plea.*

DECIDE YOUR SENTENCE

GUIDELINE FINES		
LOW INCOME	AVERAGE INCOME	HIGH INCOME
£90	£225	£540

NB. COMPENSATION - Give reasons if not awarding compensation

Remember: These are GUIDELINES not a tariff

Handling Stolen Goods

Theft Act 1968 s.22
Triable either way - see Mode of Trial Guidelines
Penalty: Level 5 and/or 6 months

CONSIDER THE SERIOUSNESS OF THE OFFENCE
(INCLUDING THE IMPACT ON THE VICTIM)

GUIDELINE: ➤   *IS COMPENSATION, DISCHARGE OR FINE APPROPRIATE?*
     IS IT SERIOUS ENOUGH FOR A COMMUNITY PENALTY?
     IS IT SO SERIOUS THAT ONLY CUSTODY IS APPROPRIATE?
     ARE MAGISTRATES' COURTS' POWERS APPROPRIATE?

 CONSIDER AGGRAVATING AND MITIGATING FACTORS ⊖

for example
- Adult involving children
- High value
- Organiser or distributor

- Offence committed on bail
- Previous convictions and failures to respond
  to previous sentences, if relevant
- *This list is not exhaustive*

for example
- For personal use
- Impulsive action
- Low value
- No financial gain
- Not part of a sophisticated operation
- Single item
- *This list is not exhaustive*

CONSIDER OFFENDER MITIGATION

for example
- Age, health (physical or mental)
- Co-operation with the police
- Voluntary compensation
- Remorse

CONSIDER YOUR SENTENCE

*Compare it with the suggested guideline level of sentence and reconsider
your reasons carefully if you have chosen a sentence at a different level.
Consider a discount for a timely guilty plea.*

DECIDE YOUR SENTENCE

NB. COMPENSATION - Give reasons if not awarding compensation

Remember: These are GUIDELINES not a tariff

Harassment, Alarm or Distress with Intent

Public Order Act 1986 s.4A
Triable only summarily
Penalty: Level 5 and/or 6 months

CONSIDER THE SERIOUSNESS OF THE OFFENCE
(INCLUDING THE IMPACT ON THE VICTIM)

IS COMPENSATION, DISCHARGE OR FINE APPROPRIATE?
IS IT SERIOUS ENOUGH FOR A COMMUNITY PENALTY?
GUIDELINE: ➤ IS IT SO SERIOUS THAT ONLY CUSTODY IS APPROPRIATE?

 CONSIDER AGGRAVATING AND MITIGATING FACTORS

for example
Racial motivation
Group action
Victims specifically targeted
High degree of planning
Night time offence
Weapon

Offence committed on bail
Previous convictions and failures to respond
to previous sentences, if relevant
This list is not exhaustive

for example
Short duration
This list is not exhaustive

CONSIDER OFFENDER MITIGATION

for example
Age, health (physical or mental)
Co-operation with the police
Voluntary compensation
Remorse

CONSIDER YOUR SENTENCE

*Compare it with the suggested guideline level of sentence and reconsider
your reasons carefully if you have chosen a sentence at a different level.
Consider a discount for a timely guilty plea.*

DECIDE YOUR SENTENCE

NB. COMPENSATION - Give reasons if not awarding compensation

Remember: These are GUIDELINES not a tariff

© The Magistrates' Association   19   Issue April 1997

Indecent Assault

Sexual Offences Act 1956 ss.14&15
Triable either way - see Mode of Trial Guidelines
Penalty: Level 5 and/or 6 months

CONSIDER THE SERIOUSNESS OF THE OFFENCE
(INCLUDING THE IMPACT ON THE VICTIM)

IS COMPENSATION, DISCHARGE OR FINE APPROPRIATE?
IS IT SERIOUS ENOUGH FOR A COMMUNITY PENALTY?
IS IT SO SERIOUS THAT ONLY CUSTODY IS APPROPRIATE?
GUIDELINE: ➤ ARE MAGISTRATES COURTS' POWERS APPROPRIATE?

CONSIDER AGGRAVATING AND MITIGATING FACTORS

for example
Vulnerable victim
Breach of trust
Age differential
Injury (may be psychiatric)
Very young victim

Offence committed on bail
Previous convictions and failures to respond
to previous sentences, if relevant
This list is not exhaustive

for example
Slight contact
This list is not exhaustive

CONSIDER OFFENDER MITIGATION

for example
Age, health (physical or mental)
Co-operation with the police
Voluntary compensation
Remorse

CONSIDER YOUR SENTENCE

*Compare it with the suggested guideline level of sentence and reconsider
your reasons carefully if you have chosen a sentence at a different level.
Consider a discount for a timely guilty plea.*

DECIDE YOUR SENTENCE

NB. COMPENSATION - Give reasons if not awarding compensation

Remember: These are GUIDELINES not a tariff

© The Magistrates' Association   20   Issue April 1997

Obstructing a Police Officer

Police Act 1996 s.89(2)
Triable only summarily
Penalty: Level 3 and/or 1 month

CONSIDER THE SERIOUSNESS OF THE OFFENCE

GUIDELINE: ➤   IS COMPENSATION, DISCHARGE OR FINE APPROPRIATE?
     IS IT SERIOUS ENOUGH FOR A COMMUNITY PENALTY?
     IS IT SO SERIOUS THAT ONLY CUSTODY IS APPROPRIATE?

 CONSIDER AGGRAVATING AND MITIGATING FACTORS

for example	for example
Racial motivation	Genuine misjudgement
Group action	Impulsive action
Premeditated	Minor obstruction
	This list is not exhaustive
Offence committed on bail	
Previous convictions and failures to respond	
to previous sentences, if relevant	
This list is not exhaustive	

CONSIDER OFFENDER MITIGATION

for example
Age, health (physical or mental)
Co-operation with the police
Remorse

CONSIDER YOUR SENTENCE

*Compare it with the suggested guideline level of sentence and reconsider
your reasons carefully if you have chosen a sentence at a different level.
Consider a discount for a timely guilty plea.*

DECIDE YOUR SENTENCE

GUIDELINE FINES		
LOW INCOME	AVERAGE INCOME	HIGH INCOME
£90	£225	£540

Remember: These are GUIDELINES not a tariff

Making off without Payment

Theft Act 1978 s.3
Triable either way - **see Mode of Trial Guidelines**
Penalty: Level 5 and/or 6 months

CONSIDER THE SERIOUSNESS OF THE OFFENCE
(INCLUDING THE IMPACT ON THE VICTIM)

GUIDELINE: ➤   IS COMPENSATION, DISCHARGE OR FINE APPROPRIATE?
     IS IT SERIOUS ENOUGH FOR A COMMUNITY PENALTY?
     IS IT SO SERIOUS THAT ONLY CUSTODY IS APPROPRIATE?
     ARE MAGISTRATES' COURTS' POWERS APPROPRIATE?

 CONSIDER AGGRAVATING AND MITIGATING FACTORS

for example	for example
Deliberate plan	Impulsive
High value	Low value
Two or more involved	*This list is not exhaustive*
Victim particularly vulnerable	
Offence committed on bail	
Previous convictions and failures to respond	
to previous sentences, if relevant	
This list is not exhaustive	

CONSIDER OFFENDER MITIGATION

for example
Age, health (physical or mental)
Co-operation with the police
Voluntary compensation
Remorse

CONSIDER YOUR SENTENCE

*Compare it with the suggested guideline level of sentence and reconsider
your reasons carefully if you have chosen a sentence at a different level.
Consider a discount for a timely guilty plea.*

DECIDE YOUR SENTENCE

GUIDELINE FINES		
LOW INCOME	AVERAGE INCOME	HIGH INCOME
£90	£225	£540

NB. COMPENSATION - Give reasons if not awarding compensation

Remember: These are GUIDELINES not a tariff

Obtaining by Deception

Theft Act 1968 s. 15
Triable either way - see Mode of Trial Guidelines
Penalty: Level 5 and/or 6 months

CONSIDER THE SERIOUSNESS OF THE OFFENCE
(INCLUDING THE IMPACT ON THE VICTIM)

IS COMPENSATION, DISCHARGE OR FINE APPROPRIATE?
IS IT SERIOUS ENOUGH FOR A COMMUNITY PENALTY?
IS IT SO SERIOUS THAT ONLY CUSTODY IS APPROPRIATE?
ARE MAGISTRATES' COURTS' POWERS APPROPRIATE?

GUIDELINE: >

 **CONSIDER AGGRAVATING AND MITIGATING FACTORS**

for example
Committed over lengthy period
Large sums or valuable goods
Two or more involved
Victim particularly vulnerable

Offence committed on bail
Previous convictions and failures to respond
to previous sentences, if relevant
This list is not exhaustive

for example
Impulsive action
Short period
Small sum
This list is not exhaustive

CONSIDER OFFENDER MITIGATION

for example
Age, health (physical or mental)
Co-operation with the police
Voluntary compensation
Remorse

CONSIDER YOUR SENTENCE

*Compare it with the suggested guideline level of sentence and reconsider
your reasons carefully if you have chosen a sentence at a different level.
Consider a discount for a timely guilty plea.*

DECIDE YOUR SENTENCE

NB. COMPENSATION - Give reasons if not awarding compensation

Remember: These are GUIDELINES not a tariff

Possession of a Bladed Instrument

Criminal Justice Act 1988 s.139
Triable either way - see Mode of Trial Guidelines
Penalty: Level 5 and/or 6 months

CONSIDER THE SERIOUSNESS OF THE OFFENCE
(INCLUDING THE IMPACT ON THE VICTIM)

IS COMPENSATION, DISCHARGE OR FINE APPROPRIATE?
IS IT SERIOUS ENOUGH FOR A COMMUNITY PENALTY?
IS IT SO SERIOUS THAT ONLY CUSTODY IS APPROPRIATE?
ARE MAGISTRATES' COURTS' POWERS APPROPRIATE?

GUIDELINE: >

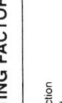 **CONSIDER AGGRAVATING AND MITIGATING FACTORS**

for example
Location of offence
Group action or joint possession
People put in fear/weapon brandished
Planned use

Offence committed on bail
Previous convictions and failures to respond
to previous sentences, if relevant
This list is not exhaustive

for example
Acting out of genuine fear
Not premeditated
This list is not exhaustive

CONSIDER OFFENDER MITIGATION

for example
Age, health (physical or mental)
Co-operation with the police
Voluntary compensation
Remorse

CONSIDER YOUR SENTENCE

*Compare it with the suggested guideline level of sentence and reconsider
your reasons carefully if you have chosen a sentence at a different level.
Consider a discount for a timely guilty plea. Consider forfeiture*

DECIDE YOUR SENTENCE

NB. COMPENSATION - Give reasons if not awarding compensation

Remember: These are GUIDELINES not a tariff

Possessing an Offensive Weapon

Prevention of Crime Act 1953 s.1
Triable either way - see Mode of Trial Guidelines
Penalty: Level 5 and/or 6 months

CONSIDER THE SERIOUSNESS OF THE OFFENCE
(INCLUDING THE IMPACT ON THE VICTIM)

IS COMPENSATION, DISCHARGE OR FINE APPROPRIATE?
IS IT SERIOUS ENOUGH FOR A COMMUNITY PENALTY?
GUIDELINE: ➢ *IS IT SO SERIOUS THAT ONLY CUSTODY IS APPROPRIATE?*
ARE MAGISTRATES' COURTS' POWERS APPROPRIATE?

 CONSIDER AGGRAVATING AND MITIGATING FACTORS

for example	for example
Location of offence	Acting out of genuine fear
Group action or joint possession	Not premeditated
People put in fear/weapon brandished	*This list is not exhaustive*
Planned use	
Offence committed on bail	
Previous convictions and failures to respond	
to previous sentences, if relevant	
This list is not exhaustive	

CONSIDER OFFENDER MITIGATION

for example
Age, health (physical or mental)
Co-operation with the police
Voluntary compensation
Remorse

CONSIDER YOUR SENTENCE

Compare it with the suggested guideline level of sentence and reconsider
your reasons carefully if you have chosen a sentence at a different level.
Consider a discount for a timely guilty plea. Consider forfeiture

DECIDE YOUR SENTENCE

NB. COMPENSATION - Give reasons if not awarding compensation

Remember: These are GUIDELINES not a tariff

Social Security - false
representation to obtain benefit

Social Security Administration Act 1992 s.112
Triable only summarily
Penalty: Level 5 and/or 3 months

CONSIDER THE SERIOUSNESS OF THE OFFENCE
(INCLUDING THE IMPACT ON THE VICTIM)

IS COMPENSATION, DISCHARGE OR FINE APPROPRIATE?
GUIDELINE: ➢ *IS IT SERIOUS ENOUGH FOR A COMMUNITY PENALTY?*
IS IT SO SERIOUS THAT ONLY CUSTODY IS APPROPRIATE?

+ CONSIDER AGGRAVATING AND MITIGATING FACTORS —

for example	for example
Fraudulent claims over a long period	Misunderstanding of regulations
Large amount	Pressurised by others
Organised group offence	Small amount
Planned deception	*This list is not exhaustive*
Offence committed on bail	
Previous convictions and failures to respond	
to previous sentences, if relevant	
This list is not exhaustive	

CONSIDER OFFENDER MITIGATION

for example
Age, health (physical or mental)
Co-operation with the police
Voluntary compensation
Remorse

CONSIDER YOUR SENTENCE

Compare it with the suggested guideline level of sentence and reconsider
your reasons carefully if you have chosen a sentence at a different level.
Consider a discount for a timely guilty plea.

DECIDE YOUR SENTENCE

NB. COMPENSATION - Give reasons if not awarding compensation

Remember: These are GUIDELINES not a tariff

Theft Act 1968 s.1
Triable either way - see Mode of Trial Guidelines
Penalty: Level 5 and/or 6 months

Theft

CONSIDER THE SERIOUSNESS OF THE OFFENCE
(INCLUDING THE IMPACT ON THE VICTIM)

GUIDELINE: ➤   IS COMPENSATION, DISCHARGE OR FINE APPROPRIATE?

         IS IT SERIOUS ENOUGH FOR A COMMUNITY PENALTY?

         IS IT SO SERIOUS THAT ONLY CUSTODY IS APPROPRIATE?

         ARE MAGISTRATES' COURTS' POWERS APPROPRIATE?

CONSIDER AGGRAVATING AND MITIGATING FACTORS

for example
High value
Planned
Sophisticated
Adult involving children
Organised team
Related damage
Vulnerable victim

Offence committed on bail
Previous convictions and failures to respond
to previous sentences, if relevant
This list is not exhaustive

for example
Impulsive action
Low value
This list is not exhaustive

CONSIDER OFFENDER MITIGATION

for example
Age, health (physical or mental)
Co-operation with the police
Voluntary compensation
Remorse

CONSIDER YOUR SENTENCE

*Compare it with the suggested guideline level of sentence and reconsider
your reasons carefully if you have chosen a sentence at a different level.
Consider a discount for a timely guilty plea.*

DECIDE YOUR SENTENCE

GUIDELINE FINES		
LOW INCOME	AVERAGE INCOME	HIGH INCOME
£135	£340	£810

NB. COMPENSATION - Give reasons if not awarding compensation
Remember: These are GUIDELINES not a tariff

Theft Act 1968 s.12
Triable only summarily
Penalty: Level 5 and/or 6 months
May disqualify

Taking Vehicle without Consent

CONSIDER THE SERIOUSNESS OF THE OFFENCE
(INCLUDING THE IMPACT ON THE VICTIM)

GUIDELINE: ➤   IS COMPENSATION, DISCHARGE OR FINE APPROPRIATE?

         IS IT SERIOUS ENOUGH FOR A COMMUNITY PENALTY?

         IS IT SO SERIOUS THAT ONLY CUSTODY IS APPROPRIATE?

CONSIDER AGGRAVATING AND MITIGATING FACTORS

for example
Group action
Premeditated
Related damage
Professional hallmarks
Vulnerable victim

Offence committed on bail
Previous convictions and failures to respond
to previous sentences, if relevant
This list is not exhaustive

for example
Misunderstanding with owner
Soon returned
Vehicle belonged to family or friend
This list is not exhaustive

CONSIDER OFFENDER MITIGATION

for example
Age, health (physical or mental)
Co-operation with the police
Voluntary compensation
Remorse

CONSIDER YOUR SENTENCE

*Compare it with the suggested guideline level of sentence and reconsider
your reasons carefully if you have chosen a sentence at a different level.
Consider a discount for a timely guilty plea.*

DECIDE YOUR SENTENCE

NB. COMPENSATION - Give reasons if not awarding compensation

Remember: These are GUIDELINES not a tariff

Theft in Breach of Trust

Theft Act 1968 s.1
Triable either way - see Mode of Trial Guidelines
Penalty: Level 5 and/or 6 months

CONSIDER THE SERIOUSNESS OF THE OFFENCE
(INCLUDING THE IMPACT ON THE VICTIM)

IS COMPENSATION, DISCHARGE OR FINE APPROPRIATE?
IS IT SERIOUS ENOUGH FOR A COMMUNITY PENALTY?
GUIDELINE: > *IS IT SO SERIOUS THAT ONLY CUSTODY IS APPROPRIATE?*
ARE MAGISTRATES' COURTS' POWERS APPROPRIATE?

 CONSIDER AGGRAVATING AND MITIGATING FACTORS ⊖

for example
Casting suspicion on others
Committed over a period
High value
Organised team
Planned
Senior employee
Sophisticated
Vulnerable victim

for example
Impulsive action
Low value
Previous inconsistent attitude by employer
Single item
Unsupported junior
This list is not exhaustive

Offence committed on bail
Previous convictions and failures to respond
to previous sentences, if relevant
This list is not exhaustive

CONSIDER OFFENDER MITIGATION

for example
Age, health (physical or mental)
Co-operation with the police
Voluntary compensation
Remorse

CONSIDER YOUR SENTENCE

Compare it with the suggested guideline level of sentence and reconsider
your reasons carefully if you have chosen a sentence at a different level.
Consider a discount for a timely guilty plea.

DECIDE YOUR SENTENCE

NB. COMPENSATION - Give reasons if not awarding compensation

Remember: These are GUIDELINES not a tariff

Threatening Behaviour

Public Order Act 1986 s.4
Triable only summarily
Penalty: Level 5 and/or 6 months

CONSIDER THE SERIOUSNESS OF THE OFFENCE
(INCLUDING THE IMPACT ON THE VICTIM)

IS COMPENSATION, DISCHARGE OR FINE APPROPRIATE?
GUIDELINE: > *IS IT SERIOUS ENOUGH FOR A COMMUNITY PENALTY?*
IS IT SO SERIOUS THAT ONLY CUSTODY IS APPROPRIATE?

 CONSIDER AGGRAVATING AND MITIGATING FACTORS ⊖

for example
Group action
People put in fear
Vulnerable victims

for example
Minor matter
Short duration
This list is not exhaustive

Offence committed on bail
Previous convictions and failures to respond
to previous sentences, if relevant
This list is not exhaustive

CONSIDER OFFENDER MITIGATION

for example
Age, health (physical or mental)
Co-operation with the police
Voluntary compensation
Remorse

CONSIDER YOUR SENTENCE

Compare it with the suggested guideline level of sentence and reconsider
your reasons carefully if you have chosen a sentence at a different level.
Consider a discount for a timely guilty plea.

DECIDE YOUR SENTENCE

NB. COMPENSATION - Give reasons if not awarding compensation

Remember: These are GUIDELINES not a tariff

TV Licence Payment Evasion

CONSIDER THE SERIOUSNESS OF THE OFFENCE
(INCLUDING THE IMPACT ON THE VICTIM)

GUIDELINE: ➤ IS COMPENSATION, DISCHARGE OR FINE APPROPRIATE?

IS IT SERIOUS ENOUGH FOR A COMMUNITY PENALTY?

(PROBATION IS ONLY AVAILABLE COMMUNITY PENALITY FOR THIS OFFENCE)

 CONSIDER AGGRAVATING AND MITIGATING FACTORS **–**

for example
Failure to respond to payment opportunities

Offence committed on bail
Previous convictions and failures to respond
to previous sentences, if relevant
This list is not exhaustive

for example
Accidental oversight
Confusion of responsibility
Licence immediately obtained
Very short unlicensed use
This list is not exhaustive

CONSIDER OFFENDER MITIGATION

for example
Age, health (physical or mental)
Co-operation with the police
Voluntary compensation
Remorse

CONSIDER YOUR SENTENCE

*Compare it with the suggested guideline level of sentence and reconsider
your reasons carefully if you have chosen a sentence at a different level.
Consider a discount for a timely guilty plea.*

DECIDE YOUR SENTENCE

GUIDELINE FINES (mono in brackets)		
LOW INCOME	AVERAGE INCOME	HIGH INCOME
£90 (£45 MONO)	£225 (£115 MONO)	£540 (£270 MONO)

NB. COMPENSATION - Give reasons if not awarding compensation
Remember: These are GUIDELINES not a tariff

Criminal Attempts Act 1981 s.9
Triable only summarily
Penalty: Level 4 and/or 3 months

Vehicle Interference

CONSIDER THE SERIOUSNESS OF THE OFFENCE
(INCLUDING THE IMPACT ON THE VICTIM)

GUIDELINE: ➤ IS COMPENSATION, DISCHARGE OR FINE APPROPRIATE?

IS IT SERIOUS ENOUGH FOR A COMMUNITY PENALTY?

IS IT SO SERIOUS THAT ONLY CUSTODY IS APPROPRIATE?

 CONSIDER AGGRAVATING AND MITIGATING FACTORS **–**

for example
Group action
Planned
Related damage

Offence committed on bail
Previous convictions and failures to respond
to previous sentences, if relevant
This list is not exhaustive

for example
Impulsive action
This list is not exhaustive

CONSIDER OFFENDER MITIGATION

for example
Age, health (physical or mental)
Co-operation with the police
Voluntary compensation
Remorse

CONSIDER YOUR SENTENCE

*Compare it with the suggested guideline level of sentence and reconsider
your reasons carefully if you have chosen a sentence at a different level.
Consider a discount for a timely plea.*

DECIDE YOUR SENTENCE

NB. COMPENSATION - Give reasons if not awarding compensation

Remember: These are GUIDELINES not a tariff

Violent Disorder

Public Order Act 1986 s.2
Triable either way - see Mode of Trial Guidelines
Penalty: Level 5 and/or 6 months

CONSIDER THE SERIOUSNESS OF THE OFFENCE
(INCLUDING THE IMPACT ON THE VICTIM)

GUIDELINE: ➤ IS COMPENSATION, DISCHARGE OR FINE APPROPRIATE?
IS IT SERIOUS ENOUGH FOR A COMMUNITY PENALTY?
IS IT SO SERIOUS THAT ONLY CUSTODY IS APPROPRIATE?
ARE MAGISTRATES' COURTS' POWERS APPROPRIATE?

➕ CONSIDER AGGRAVATING AND MITIGATING FACTORS ➖

for example
Racial motivation
Busy public place
Fighting between rival groups
Large group
People actually put in fear
Planned
Vulnerable victims
Weapon

Offence committed on bail
Previous convictions and failures to respond
to previous sentences, if relevant
This list is not exhaustive

for example
Impulsive
Nobody actually afraid
Provocation
This list is not exhaustive

CONSIDER OFFENDER MITIGATION

for example
Age, health (physical or mental)
Co-operation with the police
Voluntary compensation
Remorse

CONSIDER YOUR SENTENCE

*Compare it with the suggested guideline level of sentence and reconsider
your reasons carefully if you have chosen a sentence at a different level.
Consider a discount for a timely guilty plea.*

DECIDE YOUR SENTENCE

NB. COMPENSATION - Give reasons if not awarding compensation

Remember: These are GUIDELINES not a tariff

Wounding — Grievous Bodily Harm

Offences Against the Person Act 1861 s.20
Triable either way - see Mode of Trial Guidelines
Penalty: Level 5 and/or 6 months

CONSIDER THE SERIOUSNESS OF THE OFFENCE
(INCLUDING THE IMPACT ON THE VICTIM)

GUIDELINE: ➤ IS COMPENSATION, DISCHARGE OR FINE APPROPRIATE?
IS IT SERIOUS ENOUGH FOR A COMMUNITY PENALTY?
IS IT SO SERIOUS THAT ONLY CUSTODY IS APPROPRIATE?
ARE MAGISTRATES' COURTS' POWERS APPROPRIATE?

➕ CONSIDER AGGRAVATING AND MITIGATING FACTORS ➖

for example
Racial motivation
Deliberate kicking/biting
Extensive injuries
Group action
Offender in position of authority
Premeditated
Victim particularly vulnerable
Victim serving public
Weapon

Offence committed on bail
Previous convictions and failures to respond
to previous sentences, if relevant
This list is not exhaustive

for example
Single blow
Minor wound
Impulse
Provocation
This list is not exhaustive

CONSIDER OFFENDER MITIGATION

for example
Age, health (physical or mental)
Co-operation with the police
Voluntary compensation
Remorse

CONSIDER YOUR SENTENCE

*Compare it with the suggested guideline level of sentence and reconsider
your reasons carefully if you have chosen a sentence at a different level.
Consider a discount for a timely guilty plea.*

DECIDE YOUR SENTENCE

NB. COMPENSATION - Give reasons if not awarding compensation

Remember: These are GUIDELINES not a tariff

Criminal Justice Act 1991 sch.2
A fine - maximum £1,000
A Community Service Order (up to 60 hours)
In certain circumstances, an Attendance Centre Order
Revocation of Order and re-sentence for original offence
Commit a Crown Court Order to be dealt with at Crown Court

Breach of a community order

CONSIDER THE SERIOUSNESS OF THE OFFENCE

+ CONSIDER AGGRAVATING AND MITIGATING FACTORS ➖

for example
No attempt to start the sentence
Unco-operative
Unacceptable behaviour
This list is not exhaustive

for example
Completed a significant part of the order
This list is not exhaustive

CONSIDER OFFENDER MITIGATION
(including timely admission)

DECIDE IF THE ORDER SHOULD CONTINUE

IF THE ORDER SHOULD CONTINUE:

IS A FINE APPROPRIATE?

IS A COMMUNITY SERVICE ORDER APPROPRIATE?

WHERE THE ORDER IS A PROBATION ORDER, IS AN ATTENDANCE CENTRE ORDER APPROPRIATE?

IF THE ORDER SHOULD NOT CONTINUE AND IT IS A MAGISTRATES' COURT ORDER:

REVOKE ORDER AND RE-SENTENCE FOR ORIGINAL OFFENCE (see relevant guideline)

NB. IF THE ORDER WAS MADE BY THE CROWN COURT MAY FINE AND ALLOW ORDER TO CONTINUE OR COMMIT TO CROWN COURT TO BE DEALT WITH (CONSULT CLERK)

Remember: These are GUIDELINES not a tariff

Road Traffic Offences: Penalties

The general approach is set out in the Introduction and User Guide. However, the following notes will be of assistance when using the guidelines for road traffic offences. Always remember that these are GUIDELINES not a tariff.

Disqualification
A short period of disqualification (up to 56 days) leaves any points already on the offender's licence undisturbed. A longer period of disqualification will wipe the licence clean of penalty points.

Variable penalty points
The points awarded for a variable penalty points offence should correspond with the seriousness of the offence.

Penalty points and disqualification cannot be awarded for the same offence and the number of points or the period of disqualification suggested is targeted strictly at the seriousness of the offence and must not be reduced below the statutory minimum.

Discount for guilty plea
As is set out in the Introduction and User Guide, the precise amount of discount for a timely guilty plea will depend on the facts of each case and may be given in respect of the fine or periods of community penalty or custody.

The multiple offender
When an offender is convicted of several offences committed on one occasion, it is suggested that the court should concentrate on the most serious offence, carrying the greatest number of penalty points or period of disqualification.

The application of the totality principle may then result in less than the total of the suggested amounts of fines for the remaining individual offences.

Totting
Repeat offenders who reach 12 points within a period of three years become liable to a minimum disqualification for six months – but must be given an opportunity to address the court and/or bring evidence to show why such disqualification should not be ordered or should be reduced.

From 1 June 1997 new drivers who tot up six points or more during a two year probationary period from the date of passing the driving test (which may include points for offences committed before the test) will revert to learner status until they pass a repeat test.

Goods Vehicles 3.5 tonnes and over, buses and coaches
Penalties for offences relating to vehicles in the category involving operator licensing are now separated and divided into 3.5 tonnes to 7.5 tonnes, and 7.5 tonnes and over. Owners and drivers of such vehicles will normally be in the average or high income scale and, consequently, no low income figure is given. If, exceptionally, low income is applicable, seek documentary evidence and reduce the fine as appropriate.

It is good practice to consult the clerk, especially when issues are complex.

ROAD TRAFFIC OFFENCES INDEX

Full page guidelines identified by *

Road Traffic Act 1988 s.3
Triable only summarily
Penalty: Level 4
Must endorse (3-9 points OR may disqualify)

Careless Driving

CONSIDER THE SERIOUSNESS OF THE OFFENCE
(INCLUDING THE IMPACT ON THE VICTIM)

GUIDELINE: ➤ *IS DISCHARGE OR FINE APPROPRIATE?*

IS IT SERIOUS ENOUGH FOR A COMMUNITY PENALTY?

(PROBATION IS THE ONLY AVAILABLE COMMUNITY PENALTY FOR THIS OFFENCE)

 CONSIDER AGGRAVATING AND MITIGATING FACTORS

for example
Excessive speed
High degree of carelessness
Serious risk

Offence committed on bail
Previous convictions and failures to respond
to previous sentences, if relevant
This list is not exhaustive

for example
Sudden change in weather conditions
Minor risk
Momentary lapse
Negligible/parking damage
This list is not exhaustive

Remember: injury or damage cannot be *equated* with the degree of carelessness but may *indicate* it.

CONSIDER OFFENDER MITIGATION

for example
Co-operation with the police
Voluntary compensation
Remorse

CONSIDER YOUR SENTENCE

Endorse (3-6 points OR period of disqualification)
Consider other measures (including disqualification until test passed if appropriate)
Compare it with the suggested guideline level of sentence and reconsider
your reasons carefully if you have chosen a sentence at a different level.
Consider a discount for a timely guilty plea.

DECIDE YOUR SENTENCE

GUIDELINE FINES		
LOW INCOME	AVERAGE INCOME	HIGH INCOME
£75	£180	£450

Remember: These are GUIDELINES not a tariff

Road Traffic Act 1988 s.2
Triable either way – see Mode of Trial Guidelines
Penalty: Level 5 and/or 6 months
Must endorse and disqualify at least 12 months
Must endorse (3-11 points) if not disqualified
Must order EXTENDED re-test

Dangerous Driving

CONSIDER THE SERIOUSNESS OF THE OFFENCE
(INCLUDING THE IMPACT ON THE VICTIM)

GUIDELINE: ➤ *IS DISCHARGE OR FINE APPROPRIATE?*

IS IT SERIOUS ENOUGH FOR A COMMUNITY PENALTY?

IS IT SO SERIOUS THAT ONLY CUSTODY IS APPROPRIATE?

ARE MAGISTRATES' COURTS' POWERS APPROPRIATE?

 CONSIDER AGGRAVATING AND MITIGATING FACTORS

for example
Avoiding detection or apprehension
Competitive driving, racing, showing off
Disregard of warnings eg. from passengers
or others in vicinity
Evidence of alcohol or drugs
Excessive speed
Prolonged, persistent, deliberate bad driving
Serious risk

Offence committed on bail
Previous convictions and failures to respond
to previous sentences, if relevant
This list is not exhaustive

for example
Momentary risk not fully appreciated
No alcohol or drugs involved
Single incident
Speed not excessive
This list is not exhaustive

Remember: injury or damage cannot be *equated* with the degree of danger but may *indicate* it.

CONSIDER OFFENDER MITIGATION

for example
Co-operation with the police
Voluntary compensation
Remorse

CONSIDER YOUR SENTENCE

Endorse licence and disqualify at least 12 months unless special reasons apply.
Order EXTENDED re-test.
Compare it with the suggested guideline level of sentence and reconsider
your reasons carefully if you have chosen a sentence at a different level.
Consider a discount for a timely guilty plea.

DECIDE YOUR SENTENCE

Remember: These are GUIDELINES not a tariff

Road Traffic Act 1988 s.103
Triable only summarily
Penalty: Level 5 and/or 6 months
Must endorse: (6 points OR may further disqualify)

Driving while Disqualified by Court Order

CONSIDER THE SERIOUSNESS OF THE OFFENCE

IS DISCHARGE OR FINE APPROPRIATE?

IS IT SERIOUS ENOUGH FOR A COMMUNITY PENALTY?

GUIDELINE: ➤ *IS IT SO SERIOUS THAT ONLY CUSTODY IS APPROPRIATE?*

CONSIDER AGGRAVATING AND MITIGATING FACTORS

for example
- Efforts to avoid detection
- Long distance drive
- Planned, long term evasion
- Recently disqualified

- Offence committed on bail
- Previous convictions and failures to respond to previous sentences, if relevant
- *This list is not exhaustive*

for example
- Emergency established
- Short distance driven
- Single breach
- *This list is not exhaustive*

CONSIDER OFFENDER MITIGATION

for example
- Co-operation with the police
- Remorse

CONSIDER YOUR SENTENCE

Endorse (6 points OR period of disqualification)
Compare it with the suggested guideline level of sentence and reconsider your reasons carefully if you have chosen a sentence at a different level.
Consider a discount for a timely guilty plea.

DECIDE YOUR SENTENCE

Remember: These are GUIDELINES not a tariff

Road Traffic Act 1988 s.143
Triable only summarily
Penalty: Level 5
Must endorse (6-8 points OR may disqualify)

Driving – no insurance

CONSIDER THE SERIOUSNESS OF THE OFFENCE

GUIDELINE: ➤ *IS DISCHARGE OR FINE APPROPRIATE?*

IS IT SERIOUS ENOUGH FOR A COMMUNITY PENALTY?

(PROBATION IS THE ONLY AVAILABLE COMMUNITY PENALTY FOR THIS OFFENCE)

CONSIDER AGGRAVATING AND MITIGATING FACTORS

for example
- Deliberate driving without insurance
- LGV, HGV, PCV, PSV or minicabs
- No reference to insurance ever having been held

- Offence committed on bail
- Previous convictions and failures to respond to previous sentences, if relevant
- *This list is not exhaustive*

for example
- Accidental oversight
- Genuine mistake
- Insurance held but clearly not covering the driver or use
- Recently expired insurance
- Misled by another's error
- Responsibility for providing insurance resting with another - the parent/owner/lender/hirer
- Smaller vehicle, eg. moped
- *This list is not exhaustive*

CONSIDER OFFENDER MITIGATION

for example
- Co-operation with the police
- Remorse

CONSIDER YOUR SENTENCE

Endorse licence. *The court should have regard to the amount of the insurance premium avoided and the means of the offender and carefully consider the option of disqualification.*
Compare it with the suggested guideline level of sentence and reconsider your reasons carefully if you have chosen a sentence at a different level.
Consider a discount for a timely guilty plea.

DECIDE YOUR SENTENCE

GUIDELINE FINES		
LOW INCOME	AVERAGE INCOME	HIGH INCOME
£215 (£300 LGV/PCV)	£540 (£750 LGV/PCV)	£1,300 (£1,800 LGV/PCV)

Remember: These are GUIDELINES not a tariff

Excess Alcohol (Drive or attempt to drive)

Road Traffic Act s.5 (1)(a)
Penalty: Level 5 and/or 6 months: Triable only summarily
Must endorse and disqualify at least 12 months; disqualify at least 36 months for a further offence within 10 years

CONSIDER THE SERIOUSNESS OF THE OFFENCE
The level of seriousness and guideline sentence is related to the breath/blood/urine reading

+ CONSIDER AGGRAVATING AND MITIGATING FACTORS

for example
Police chase
Caused injury/fear/damage
Type of vehicle, eg. carrying passengers for reward/large goods vehicle
Evidence of nature of the driving
High reading (and in combination with above)
Ability to drive seriously impaired

Offence committed on bail
Previous convictions and failures to respond to previous sentences, if relevant
This list is not exhaustive

for example
Spiked drinks
Moving a vehicle a very short distance
This list is not exhaustive

BREATH	BLOOD	URINE	DISQUALIFY	GUIDELINE	LOW INCOME	AVERAGE INCOME	HIGH INCOME
36-55	80-125	107-170	12 months	FINE	£180	£450	£1,080
56-70	126-160	171-214	18 months	FINE	£240	£600	£1,440
71-85	161-195	215-260	24 months	FINE	£300	£750	£1,800
86-100	196-229	261-308	24 months	CONSIDER COMMUNITY PENALTY			
101-115	230-264	309-354	30 months				
116-130	285-300	355-400	30 months	CONSIDER CUSTODY			
131+	301+	401+	36 months				

CONSIDER OFFENDER MITIGATION
for example
Co-operation with the police

CONSIDER YOUR SENTENCE
Compare it with the suggested guideline level of sentence and reconsider your reasons carefully if you have chosen a sentence at a different level.
Consider a discount for a timely guilty plea.

DECIDE YOUR SENTENCE

Remember: These are GUIDELINES not a tariff

Refuse evidential specimen (Drive or attempt to drive)

Road Traffic Act s.7 (6)
Penalty: Level 5 and/or 6 months: Triable only summarily
Must endorse and disqualify at least 12 months; disqualify at least 36 months for a further offence within 10 years

CONSIDER THE SERIOUSNESS OF THE OFFENCE

GUIDELINE: >
IS DISCHARGE OR FINE APPROPRIATE?
IS IT SERIOUS ENOUGH FOR A COMMUNITY PENALTY?
IS IT SO SERIOUS THAT ONLY CUSTODY IS APPROPRIATE?

+ CONSIDER AGGRAVATING AND MITIGATING FACTORS

for example
Police chase
Caused injury/fear/damage
Type of vehicle, eg. carrying passengers for reward/large goods vehicle
Evidence of nature of the driving
Ability to drive seriously impaired

Offence committed on bail
Previous convictions and failures to respond to previous sentences, if relevant
This list is not exhaustive

for example
Moving a vehicle a very short distance
This list is not exhaustive

CONSIDER OFFENDER MITIGATION
for example
Voluntary completion of alcohol impaired driver course (if available)
Remorse

CONSIDER YOUR SENTENCE
Endorse licence. DISQUALIFY — a minimum period of 18 months is suggested.
Examine carefully aggravating/mitigating factors disclosed - do these justify any variation in period of disqualification suggested? If substantial aggravating factors, consider higher fine/community penalty/custody.
Compare it with the suggested guideline level of sentence and reconsider your reasons carefully if you have chosen a sentence at a different level.
Consider a discount for a timely guilty plea.

DECIDE YOUR SENTENCE

GUIDELINE FINES		
LOW INCOME	AVERAGE INCOME	HIGH INCOME
£240	£600	£1,440

Remember: These are GUIDELINES not a tariff

Fraudulent use etc.
Vehicle Excise Licence etc.

Vehicle Excise and Registration Act 1994 s.44
Triable either way - see Mode of Trial Guidelines
Penalty: Level 5

CONSIDER THE SERIOUSNESS OF THE OFFENCE

GUIDELINE: ➤   **IS DISCHARGE OR FINE APPROPRIATE?**

    IS IT SERIOUS ENOUGH FOR A COMMUNITY PENALTY?

    (PROBATION IS ONLY AVAILABLE COMMUNITY PENALTY FOR THIS OFFENCE)

 ## CONSIDER AGGRAVATING AND MITIGATING FACTORS   ⚊

for example
- Deliberately planned
- Disc forged or altered
- Long term defrauding
- LGV, HGV, PCV, PSV taxi or private hire vehicle

- Offence committed on bail
- Previous convictions and failures to respond to previous sentences, if relevant
- *This list is not exhaustive*

for example
- Impulsive action
- *This list is not exhaustive*

CONSIDER OFFENDER MITIGATION

for example
- Co-operation with the police/DVLA
- Remorse

CONSIDER YOUR SENTENCE

Compare it with the suggested guideline level of sentence and reconsider your reasons carefully if you have chosen a sentence at a different level.
Consider a discount for a timely guilty plea.

DECIDE YOUR SENTENCE

	GUIDELINE FINES	
LOW INCOME	AVERAGE INCOME	HIGH INCOME
£100	£240	£575

Remember: These are GUIDELINES not a tariff

Failing to Stop
Failing to Report

Road Traffic Act 1988 s. 170 (4)
Triable only summarily
Penalty: Level 5 and/or 6 months
Must endorse: (5-10 points OR disqualify)

CONSIDER THE SERIOUSNESS OF THE OFFENCE
(INCLUDING THE IMPACT ON THE VICTIM)

GUIDELINE: ➤   **IS COMPENSATION, DISCHARGE OR FINE APPROPRIATE?**

    IS IT SERIOUS ENOUGH FOR A COMMUNITY PENALTY?

    IS IT SO SERIOUS THAT ONLY CUSTODY IS APPROPRIATE?

 ## CONSIDER AGGRAVATING AND MITIGATING FACTORS   ⚊

for example
- Evidence of drinking
- Serious injury and failure to stop or remain at scene
- Serious injury and/or serious damage

- Offence committed on bail
- Previous convictions and failures to respond to previous sentences, if relevant
- *This list is not exhaustive*

for example
- Believed identity to be known
- Failed to stop but reported
- Genuine fear of retribution
- Negligible damage
- No one at scene but failed to report
- Stayed at scene but failed to give/left before giving full particulars
- *This list is not exhaustive*

CONSIDER OFFENDER MITIGATION

for example
- Co-operation with the police
- Voluntary compensation
- Remorse

CONSIDER YOUR SENTENCE

Endorse (5-10 points OR period of disqualification)
Compare it with the suggested guideline level of sentence and reconsider your reasons carefully if you have chosen a sentence at a different level.
Consider a discount for a timely guilty plea.

DECIDE YOUR SENTENCE

	GUIDELINE FINES	
LOW INCOME	AVERAGE INCOME	HIGH INCOME
£145	£360	£865

Remember: These are GUIDELINES not a tariff

Road Traffic Act 1984 s.89(1)
Triable only summarily
Penalty: Level 3 (Level 4 if motorway)
Must endorse (3-6 points OR may disqualify)

Speeding

CONSIDER THE SERIOUSNESS OF THE OFFENCE

GUIDELINE: ➤   *IS DISCHARGE OR FINE APPROPRIATE?*

(+) CONSIDER AGGRAVATING AND MITIGATING FACTORS

for example
LGV, HGV, PCV or minicab
Location/time of day/visibility
Serious risk
Towing caravan/trailer

Offence committed on bail
Previous convictions and failures to respond to previous sentences, if relevant
This list is not exhaustive

for example
Emergency established
Limit change (eg. 40 to 30 mph)
This list is not exhaustive

GUIDELINE FINES

GUIDELINE PENALTY POINTS	LEGAL SPEED LIMITS	EXCESS SPEED — MPH	LOW INCOME	AVERAGE INCOME	HIGH INCOME
3	20-30 mph	Up to 10 mph	£60	£150	£360
	40-50 mph	Up to 15 mph			
	60-70 mph	Up to 20 mph			
4 or 5	20-30 mph	From 11-20	£90	£225	£540
	40-50 mph	From 16-25			
	60-70 mph	From 21-30			
6 or disqualify (14-56 days)	20-30 mph	From 21-30	£135	£335	£810
	40-50 mph	From 26-35			
	60-70 mph	From 31-40			

CONSIDER OFFENDER MITIGATION

for example
Co-operation with the police
Fixed penalty not taken up for valid reason

CONSIDER YOUR SENTENCE
Endorse (3-6 points OR period of disqualification)
Consider other measures (including disqualification until test passed if appropriate)
Compare it with the suggested guideline level of sentence and reconsider your reasons carefully if you have chosen a sentence at a different level.
Consider a discount for a timely guilty plea.

DECIDE YOUR SENTENCE

Remember: These are GUIDELINES not a tariff

Offences considered appropriate for guideline of discharge or fine, other than in exceptional circumstances

	PENALTY POINTS	MAXIMUM PENALTY	LOW INCOME	AVERAGE INCOME	HIGH INCOME
ALCHOHOL/DRUGS					
In charge whilst unfit through drink/drugs or refusing evidential specimen. *Consider disqualification if evidence of driving or other aggravating factor*	10*	Level 4 and/or 3 months E	£145	£360	£865
Refusing roadside breath test	4	Level 3 E	£75	£180	£450
DOCUMENTS - Fail to produce	-	Level 3	£25	£60	£145
DRIVER					
Not supplying details *If company- owned use high income fine when unable to apply endorsement*	3*	Level 3 E	£85	£210	£500*
LICENCE OFFENCES					
† No driving licence, where could be covered	-	Level 3	£15	£30	£75
† Excise Licence not displayed	-	Level 3	£15	£30	£75
LIGHTS - Driving without	-	Level 3	£40	£90	£210
OWNERSHIP - Not notifying DVLA of change, etc.	-	Level 3	£60	£150	£360
PARKING OFFENCES					
† Dangerous Position	3	Level 3 E	£60	£150	£360
† Obstruction	-	Level 3	£25	£60	£145
† Pelican/zebra crossing	3	Level 3 E	£60	£150	£360
† Stopping on clearway	-	Level 3	£40	£90	£210
PROVISIONAL LICENCE OFFENCES					
† Not in accordance with licence	3	Level 3 E	£60	£150	£360
TEST CERTIFICATE - Not held	-	Level 3	£40	£90	£210
TRAFFIC DIRECTION OFFENCES					
† Fail to comply with height restriction	3	Level 3 E	£60	£150	£360
† Fail to comply with red traffic light	3	Level 3 E	£60	£150	£360
† Fail to comply with stop sign/double white lines	3	Level 3 E	£60	£150	£360
† Fail to give precedence - pelican/zebra crossing	3	Level 3 E	£60	£150	£360
TRAFFIC OR POLICE SIGNS (non endorsable)					
† Fail to comply	-	Level 3	£40	£90	£210

† All these items are eligible for fixed penalty offer. If fixed penalty was offered, consider any reasons for not taking up and, if valid, fine amount of appropriate fixed penalty and endorse if required, considering whether costs be waived and allow a maximum of 28 days to pay. Or, if fixed penalty refused or not offered, consider whether known circumstances merit any discount for a guilty plea (but not normally below the fixed penalty amount) or if there are aggravating factors which merit increasing the fine.

In all cases, consider the safety factor, damage to roads, commercial gain and, if driver is not the owner, with whom prime responsibility should lie.

E: Must ENDORSE (unless special reasons) and may disqualify

Remember: These are GUIDELINES not a tariff

Offences relating to goods vehicles, buses and coaches from 3.5 tonnes up to 7.5 tonnes gross

	PENALTY POINTS	MAXIMUM PENALTY	OPERATOR	DRIVER AVERAGE INCOME	DRIVER HIGH INCOME
DEFECTS					
Brakes	3	Level 5 E	£600	£200	£480
Steering	3	Level 5 E	£600	£200	£480
Tyres (each)	3	Level 5 E	£600	£200	£480
Loss of wheel	3	Level 5 E	£1,200	£400	£960
Exhaust emission	-	Level 4	£375	£120	£300
Other offences	-	Level 4	£300	£100	£240
LOADS					
Condition of vehicle/accessories/equipment	3	Level 5 E	£750	£240	£600
Purpose of use/number of passengers/how carried	3	Level 5 E	£750	£240	£600
Weight, position or distribution of load	3	Level 5 E	£750	£240	£600
Insecure load	3	Level 5 E	£750	£240	£600
Overloading or exceeding maximum axle weight	-	Level 5	£750*	£240*	£600*
			*Plus increase in proportion to percentage of overloading		
OPERATORS LICENCE					
Not held	-	Level 4	£600	£200	£480
TACHOGRAPH					
Not fitted	-	Level 5	£600	£200	£480
Not properly used	-	Level 5	£600	£200	£480
Falsification/Fraudulent use	-	Level 5	£900	£300	£720

Drivers of these vehicles will normally be in the average or high income scale and, consequently, no low income figure is given. If, exceptionally, low income is applicable, seek documentary evidence and reduce the fine as appropriate

E: Must ENDORSE (unless special reasons) and may disqualify

Remember: These are GUIDELINES not a tariff

Offences considered appropriate for guideline of discharge or fine, other than in exceptional circumstances

	PENALTY POINTS	MAXIMUM PENALTY	LOW INCOME	AVERAGE INCOME	HIGH INCOME
VEHICLE DEFECTS ETC UP TO 3.5 TONNES GROSS VEHICLE WEIGHT					
Defects					
† Brakes/Steering/Tyres (each)	3	Level 4 E	£60	£150	£360
† Loss of wheel	3	Level 4 E	£120	£300	£720
† Exhaust emission	-	Level 3	£40	£90	£240
† Other offences	-	Level 3	£30	£75	£180
Loads, danger of injury by:					
† Condition of vehicle/accessories/equipment	3	Level 4 E	£75	£180	£450
† Purpose of use/passenger numbers/how carried	3	Level 4 E	£75	£180	£450
† Weight, position or distribution of load	3	Level 4 E	£75	£180	£450
† Insecure load	3	Level 4 E	£75	£180	£450
* Overloading or exceeding maximum axle weight	-	Level 5	£75*	£180*	£450*
			Plus increase in proportion to percentage of overloading		

Examine carefully evidence of responsibility for overload and, if commercial gain relates to owner, consider doubling these figures

† All these items are eligible for fixed penalty offer. If fixed penalty was offered, consider any reasons for not taking up and, if valid, fine amount of appropriate fixed penalty and endorse if required, considering whether costs be waived and allow a maximum of 28 days to pay. Or, if fixed penalty refused or not offered, consider whether known circumstances merit any discount for a guilty plea (but not normally below the fixed penalty amount) or if there are aggravating factors which merit increasing the fine.

In all cases, consider the safety factor; damage to roads, commercial gain and, if driver is not the owner, with whom prime responsibility should lie.

E: Must ENDORSE (unless special reasons) and may disqualify

Remember: These are GUIDELINES not a tariff

Motorway Offences

	PENALTY POINTS	MAXIMUM PENALTY	LOW INCOME	AVERAGE INCOME	HIGH INCOME
DRIVING					
† Driving in reverse on motorway	3	Level 4 E	£145	£360	£865
† Driving in reverse on sliproad	3	Level 4 E	£50	£120	£300
† Driving in wrong direction on motorway · Consider disqualification	3*	Level 4 E	£240	£600	£1,440
† Driving in wrong direction on sliproad	3	Level 4 E	£75	£180	£450
† Driving off carriageway - central reservation	3	Level 4 E	£75	£180	£450
† Driving off carriageway - hard shoulder	3	Level 4 E	£60	£150	£360
† Driving on sliproad against no entry sign	3	Level 4 E	£75	£180	£450
* Making U-Turn. · Consider disqualification	3*	Level 4 E	£200	£500	£1,200
LEARNERS					
† Learner driver or excluded vehicle	3	Level 4 E	£75	£180	£450
STOPPING					
† Stopping on hard shoulder of motorway	-	Level 4	£50	£120	£300
† Stopping on hard shoulder of sliproad	-	Level 4	£25	£60	£145
THIRD LANE					
† Vehicle over 7.5 tonnes or drawing trailer in third lane	3	Level 4 E	£120	£300	£720
WALKING					
† Walking on motorway or sliproad	-	Level 4	£40	£90	£210
† Walking on hard shoulder or verge	-	Level 4	£25	£60	£145

† All these items are eligible for fixed penalty offer. If fixed penalty was offered, consider any reasons for not taking up and, if valid, fine amount of appropriate fixed penalty and endorse if required, considering whether costs be waived and allow a maximum of 28 days to pay. Or, if fixed penalty refused or not offered, consider whether known circumstances merit any discount for a guilty plea (but not normally below the fixed penalty amount) or if there are aggravating factors which merit increasing the fine.

In all cases, consider the safety factor, damage to roads, commercial gain and, if driver is not the owner, with whom prime responsibility should lie.

E: Must ENDORSE (unless special reasons) and may disqualify

Remember: These are GUIDELINES not a tariff

Offences relating to goods vehicles, buses and coaches 7.5 tonnes gross and over

	PENALTY POINTS	MAXIMUM PENALTY	OPERATOR	DRIVER	
				AVERAGE INCOME	HIGH INCOME
DEFECTS					
Brakes	3	Level 5 E	£600	£200	£480
Steering	3	Level 5 E	£600	£200	£480
Tyres (each)	3	Level 5 E	£600	£200	£480
Loss of wheel	3	Level 5 E	£1,200	£400	£960
Exhaust emission	-	Level 4	£375	£120	£300
Other offences	-	Level 4	£300	£100	£240
LOADS					
Condition of vehicle/accessories/equipment	3	Level 5 E	£900	£300	£720
Purpose of use/number of passengers/how carried	3	Level 5 E	£900	£300	£720
Weight, position or distribution of load	3	Level 5 E	£900	£300	£720
Insecure load	3	Level 5 E	£900	£300	£720
Overloading or exceeding maximum axle weight	-	Level 5	£900*	£300*	£720*
			*Plus increase in proportion to percentage of overloading		
OPERATORS LICENCE					
Not held	-	Level 4	£750	£240	£600
SPEED LIMITERS					
Not fitted	-	Level 5	£375	£120	£300
Not properly used or incorrectly calibrated	-	Level 5	£450	£150	£360
TACHOGRAPH					
Not fitted	-	Level 5	£600	£200	£480
Not properly used	-	Level 5	£600	£200	£480
Falsification/Fraudulent use	-	Level 5	£900	£300	£720

Drivers of these vehicles will normally be in the average or high income scale and, consequently, no low income figure is given. If, exceptionally, low income is applicable, seek documentary evidence and reduce the fine as appropriate.

E: Must ENDORSE (unless special reasons) and may disqualify

Remember: These are GUIDELINES not a tariff

Offence codes—Endorsements and disqualification

Where a court orders a driving licence to be endorsed and/or an offender to be disqualified the details of the offences are coded. The codes appear on driving licences and DVLA printouts: see, generally, *Chapter 7*. The codes are normally abbreviations of the names of offences, eg SP = speeding, CD = careless driving. The full list of offence codes (March 1998) is as follows:

CODE   OFFENCE   POINTS

Offences in Relation to Accidents

CODE	OFFENCE	POINTS
AC10	Failing to stop after an accident	5-10
AC20	Failing to give particulars or to report an accident within 24 hours	5-10
AC30	Undefined accident offence	4-9

Driving Whilst Disqualified

CODE	OFFENCE	POINTS
BA10	Driving whilst disqualified by order of the court	6
BA20	Driving while disqualified as under age	Replaced by LC20 from 1 July 1992
BA30	Attempting to drive while disqualified by order of court	6

Careless Driving Offences

CODE	OFFENCE	POINTS
CD10	Driving without due care and attention	3-9
CD20	Driving without reasonable consideration for other road users	3-9
CD30	Driving without due care and attention or without reasonable consideration for other road users	3-9 3-9
CD40	Causing death by careless driving when unfit through drink	3-11*
CD50	Causing death by careless driving when unfit through drugs	3-11*
CD60	Causing death by careless driving with alcohol level above the limit	3-11*
CD70	Causing death by careless driving then failing to provide specimen for analysis	3-11*

CODE   OFFENCE   POINTS

Construction and Use Offences (Vehicles or Parts)

CU10	Using a vehicle with defective brakes	3
CU20	Causing or likely to cause danger by reason or use of unsuitable vehicle or using a vehicle with parts or accessories (excluding brakes, steering or tyres) in dangerous conditions	3
CU30	Using a vehicle with defective tyres	3
CU40	Using a vehicle with defective steering	3
CU50	Causing or likely to cause danger by reason of load or passengers	)
CU60	Undefined failure to comply with construction and use regulation	) Rescinded) 1 July 1992)

Dangerous (Formerly Reckless) Driving Offences

DD30	Reckless driving	Replaced by DD 40 from 1 July 1992
DD40	Dangerous driving	3-11*
DD60	Manslaughter or, in Scotland, culpable homicide while driving a motor vehicle	3-11*
DD70	Causing death by reckless driving	Replaced by DD80 from 1 July 1992
DD80	Causing death by dangerous driving	3-11*

Drink or Drugs Offences

DR10	Driving or attempting to drive with alcohol concentration above limit	3-11*
DR20	Driving or attempting to drive when unfit through drink	3-11*
DR30	Driving or attempting to drive then refusing to provide specimen for analysis	3-11* 3-11*
DR40	In charge of a vehicle with alcohol concentration above limit	10
DR50	In charge of a vehicle when unfit through drink	10
DR60	Failure to provide a specimen for analysis (other than driving or attempting to drive)	10
DR70	Failing to provide specimen for breath test	4
DR80	Driving or attempting to drive when unfit through drugs	3-11*
DR90	In charge of a vehicle when unfit through drugs	10

CODE   OFFENCE   POINTS

Insurance Offences

| IN10 | Using vehicle uninsured against third party risks | 6-8 |

Licence Offences

LC10	Driving without a licence	Replaced by LC20 from 1 July 1992
LC20	Driving otherwise than in accordance with a licence	3-6
LC30	Driving after making a false declaration about fitness when applying for a licence	3-6
LC40	Driving a vehicle having failed to notify a disability	3-6
LC50	Driving after a licence has been revoked or refused on medical grounds	3-6

Miscellaneous Offences

MS10	Leaving vehicle in dangerous position	3
MS20	Unlawful pillion riding	3
MS30	Play street offence	2
MS40	Driving with uncorrected defective eyesight or refusing to submit to eyesight test	3 (See MS70 and MS80)
MS50	Motor racing on the highway	3-11*
MS60	Offences not covered by other codes as appropriate	
MS70	Driving with uncorrected defective eyesight	3
MS80	Refusing to submit to an eyesight test	3
MS90	Failure to give information as to identity of driver in certain cases	3

Motorway Offences

| MW10 | Contravention of special roads regulations (excluding speed limits) | 3 |

Pedestrian Crossing Offences

PC10	Undefined contravention of pedestrian crossing regulations	3 (mainly Scottish courts)
PC20	Contravention of pedestrian crossing regulations with moving vehicle	3
PC30	Contravention of pedestrian crossing regulations with stationary vehicle	3

CODE   OFFENCE   POINTS

PL10	Driving without L-plates	)	
PL20	Not accompanied by a qualified person	)	Replaced by
PL30	Carrying a person not qualified	)	LC 20
PL40	Drawing an unauthorised trailer	)	from 1 July 92
PL50	Undefined failure to comply with	)	
	the conditions of a provisional licence	)	

Speed Limits Offences

SP10	Exceeding goods vehicle speed limit	3-6
SP20	Exceeding speed limit for type of vehicle (excluding goods/passenger vehicles)	3-6
SP30	Exceeding statutory speed limit on a public road	3-6
SP40	Exceeding passenger vehicle speed limit	3-6
SP50	Exceeding speed limit on a motorway	3-6
SP60	Undefined speed limit offence	3-6

Traffic Directions and Signs Offences

TS10	Failing to comply with traffic light signals	3
TS20	Failing to comply with double white lines	3
TS30	Failing to comply with a 'stop' sign	3
TS40	Failing to comply with directions of a constable or traffic warden	3
TS50	Failing to comply with a traffic sign (except stop signs, traffic lights or double white lines)	3
TS60	Failing to comply with school crossing patrol sign	3
TS70	Undefined failure to comply with a traffic direction or sign	3

Offences of Theft or Unauthorised Taking

UT10	Taking and driving away a vehicle without consent or an attempt thereat (in England and Wales prior to Theft Act 1968 only). Driving a vehicle knowing it to have been taken without consent; allowing oneself to	))))))	no longer endorsable since 1 July 1992

	be carried in or on a vehicle knowing	)	
	it to have been taken without consent.	)	As above
	(primarily for use by Scottish courts)	)	
UT20	Stealing or attempting to steal a vehicle	))	
UT30	Going equipped for stealing or taking a motor vehicle	))	
UT40	Taking or attempting to take a vehicle without consent. Driving or	))	Non-
	attempting to drive a vehicle knowing	)	endorsable
	it to have been taken without consent.)	)	
	Allowing oneself to be carried in or	)	
	on a vehicle knowing it to have been	)	
	taken without consent	)	
UT50	Aggravated taking of a vehicle		3-11*

SPECIAL CODE: TT99
Only used to indicate a disqualification under the totting-up procedures.

SPECIAL CODE NE99
Used where points or disqualification still relevant but endorsement no longer applicable.

AIDING, ABETTING, COUNSELLING, PROCURING
Coded as above but with zero changed to 2 eg UT10 becomes UT12.

CAUSING OR PERMITTING
Coded as above but with zero changed to 4 eg PL10 becomes PL14.

INCITING
Coded as above but with zero changed to 6 eg DD30 becomes DD36.

---

* These offences involve mandatory disqualification except where special reasons are found by the court. The offences then carry 'notional points' — on a range from 3 to 11 — ie which are imposed if special reasons *are* found: see generally *Chapter 7*.

EQUAL TREATMENT IN COURTS

All magistrates take the judicial oath to '. . . do right to all manner of people'. Of course, no-one can guarantee that they will not insult someone completely unintentionally, or that they will never convey an impression of unfair treatment. But the desire not to cause offence to court users and to appear to be acting fairly—as well as in fact doing so—are important considerations for anyone sitting in judgment upon other people.

The following notes seek to provide a broad reminder of items that magistrates need to be aware of in order to reinforce efforts to ensure that no-one leaves court feeling that he or she has been unfairly treated because of his or her gender, race, religion, disability (or for any other reason):

- **listen carefully** to what witnesses/defendants call themselves. To many people their name and whether they are addressed as 'Miss' or 'Mrs' or 'Dr' is important. If in doubt, and the name or designation is relevant, ask the individual how they would like to be addressed, or how they pronounce their name.
- **don't make assumptions** about people based on their gender, race, disability, religion or occupation.
- **avoid using inappropriate terminology** such as 'My dear', or referring to someone of mixed ethnic origin as 'half-caste', 'coloured'.
- **avoid making jokes** particularly at the expense of someone appearing before the court, or humorous remarks based upon someone's gender, racial origin or physical characteristics.

Points to Remember

- Generally speaking, people appreciate being addressed accurately and appropriately.
- It is through words that we express how we think and feel.
- The inadvertent use of inappropriate words may cause offence.
- Some words or phrases which may have been acceptable in the past are no longer acceptable today.

Some Further Considerations

Magistrates have a general duty to act fairly, impartially and without bias—in accordance with the principles of 'natural justice'. Research and experience indicate that through lack of understanding people can give the impression of being discriminatory despite their best intentions or efforts. In one Court of Appeal ruling a Crown Court judge was reported to have said:

> You are four coloured men. I do not want you to think for one moment that if you were four white men standing here you would be getting a moment less by way of sentence than you in fact will get. You are being sentenced for robbery not for the colour of your skin.

Leaving aside the fact that the description 'coloured' is nowadays considered unacceptable, Lord Justice Roch said

> No doubt this was well intentioned but [the judge] should not have said it. The colour, race, or religion of defendants was wholly irrelevant because all were equal in the eyes of the law, the only exception being made in the case of a public order offence which was racially motivated.

Section 95 Criminal Justice Act 1991

Section 95 reinforces common law principles by requiring the Home Secretary to publish each year such information as he considers expedient for the purposes of facilitating the performance by persons engaged in the administration of criminal justice of their duty to avoid discriminating against any person on the ground of race, sex or any other improper ground. Publications stemming from this provision include: *Race and Criminal Justice* (1992), *Gender and the Criminal Justice System* (1992), *Digest: Information on the Criminal Justice System in England and Wales* (1993) and *Race and the Criminal Justice System* (1994). Other initiatives include:

- The creation of a Judicial Studies Board Ethnic Minorities Advisory Committee which has encouraged the development of a training pack for new lay magistrates.
- The Justices' Clerks' Society has published two papers designed to promote equality: *Dealing with Disadvantage* (1993) and *Black People in Magistrates' Courts* (1995).
- All the main agencies involved in court work have introduced procedures and initiatives to combat discrimination. Thus, eg the probation service has taken steps to promote racial equality in all aspects of its work, including the production of policy statements and guidance. This extends to the monitoring of pre-sentence reports.

Such initiatives are increasing as people become more aware of discrimination issues generally. Knowledge of such matters and an awareness of their implications are of considerable importance to sentencers and deserve a high priority.

Recommended Further Reading

Race and Religion: A Brief Guide for Magistrates' Courts, The Justices' Clerks' Society and NACRO.

Judicial Studies Board Papers:

- Terms and Terminology
- Names and Naming Systems
- Oaths and Oath Taking.

These three papers are available from the Judicial Studies Board, 9th Floor, Millbank Tower, Millbank, London SW1 4QP.

FINANCIAL IMPLICATIONS OF DECISIONS

Section 95 also deals with the financial implications of sentencing decisions. Whilst not, conventionally, a relevant consideration in arriving at an appropriate sentence: see, generally, *Chapter 2*), section 95 created a mechanism for magistrates (alongside other people involved in the administration of justice) to be supplied with information about the financial implications of their decisions. Under this provision, the Home Secretary must 'publish each year such information as he considers expedient' for this purpose. The latest fully comparative figures are for 1996/7 when weekly costs per offender were:

- local prison: £421
- young offender institution: £344
- community service order: £33
- probation order: £42
- supervision order: £37
- combination order: £62
- attendance centre: average *total cost* of order £185.

The assistance of Terry Moore, Justices' Clerk, Woodspring, with preparation of *Appendix E* is gratefully acknowledged.

The Sentence of the Court deals only with *adult* offenders, ie people aged 18 and over. Those below that age ('youths') are sub-divided into:

- 'children': aged 10 to 13 years inclusive; and
- 'young persons': aged 14 to 17 years inclusive

and normally appear in the youth court.[1] They may, however, sometimes appear in the ordinary magistrates' court, most frequently:

- for remand (often a 'first remand' if no youth court is sitting)
- when jointly charged with someone aged 18 or over
- when charged with aiding, abetting, counselling, procuring, allowing or permitting an offence alleged against a person aged 18 or over (or vice versa, ie the adult may be the abettor)
- when charged with an offence arising out of circumstances which are the same as or connected with those giving rise to an offence with which a person aged 18 years or over is charged.

If convicted, the magistrates' court must normally remit the offender to the youth court for sentence but in certain circumstances it may decide to retain jurisdiction when its sentencing powers are restricted to:

- an absolute discharge or a conditional discharge
- a fine (subject to special maxima 📖✋)
- binding over the parent or guardian
- any appropriate ancillary orders, eg compensation, endorsement, forfeiture.

There is merit in remitting a case to the youth court after conviction unless the outcome is clearly straightforward.[2] Among other considerations:

- youth court magistrates receive special training
- the sentencing powers of the youth court
  —are more flexible; and
  —specifically designed for a younger age group

---

[1] For a general outline of youth justice, see *Introduction to the Youth Court,* Waterside Press.

[2] For even stronger reasons after the changes proposed in the Crime and Disorder Bill (1997) it seems.

- the 'welfare principle' in the Children and Young Persons Act 1933—to which youth courts are attuned—is often difficult to reconcile with the underlying 'just deserts' approach to sentencing. *All courts* are required to have regard to the 1933 Act which states:

> Every court in dealing with a child or young person who is brought before it, either as an offender or otherwise, shall have regard to the welfare of the child or young person, and shall in a proper case take steps for removing him from undesirable surroundings, and for securing that proper provision is made for his education and training.

- the rules for pre-sentence reports (PSRs) are stricter in relation to youths—meaning that in practice there will often need to be an adjournment anyway.

However, there may be occasions when jurisdiction can reasonably be retained by the adult court, especially if the youth and the adult are very close in age and it is felt that one bench should sentence both. Generally speaking, advice is prudent due to these and other special considerations such as 'parental responsibility' for the payment of fines and compensation (which differs according to whether the youth is aged 15 years of age or less), the practical implications of binding over a parent, or the interaction of the two jurisdictions. 📖 ✋

A note on publicity
The press is severely restricted concerning what can be reported from the *youth court*. Similarly, when a youth appears in the *adult court* (in whatever capacity) that court may wish to consider using a discretionary power to impose restrictions. 📖 ✋

Anyone who has been convicted and sentenced by a magistrates' court can appeal to the Crown Court against the conviction, sentence, or both or to the High Court on a point of law. The prosecutor cannot appeal against an acquittal, or against what he or she believes to be an over-lenient sentence (a form of appeal currently restricted to certain sentences imposed by the Crown Court).

APPEAL TO THE CROWN COURT

This is the normal method. The convicted person must give notice of appeal within 21 days of being sentenced. This can be extended by the Crown Court (called 'leave to appeal out of time'). The notice of appeal must set out the details of the conviction and sentence and state the grounds of appeal.

Against conviction

Appeals against conviction are heard by a judge sitting with two magistrates (usually: technically there can be up to four magistrates). There is no jury. The case is heard afresh. The Crown Court either upholds the conviction or substitutes an acquittal. If it convicts, it also proceeds to sentence.

Against sentence

This is also heard by a judge and two magistrates. The court is addressed by the appellant (ie the person making the appeal) or his or her legal representative. The Crown Court can confirm the decision or substitute its own sentence, either a more severe or a lesser one—but limited to magistrates' maximum powers of punishment.

APPEAL TO THE DIVISIONAL COURT

Appeals on points of law go to the Queen's Bench Division (QBD) of the High Court of Justice—where they are heard by a 'Divisional Court' of the QBD. There are three methods:

Case stated

Here, the magistrates state a case for the opinion of the High Court. This involves setting down in writing what facts the magistrates found to exist in the case and saying what law or principles they applied to those facts. The Divisional Court either upholds the magistrates' decision or makes some other order, eg quashing the conviction; or ordering the magistrates to rehear the case applying the law correctly. There is a timetable for the various stages. The process starts with an application by *either* party for the magistrates to state a case for the opinion of the High Court—which must be made within 21 days of the final decision by the magistrates court. Magistrates can refuse a 'frivolous' application, or ask the applicant to identify the point of law involved, eg where they are unable to discern a legal issue which actually bore on the decision.

Judicial review

Anyone who is aggrieved by a decision of magistrates (which can extend beyond the parties to other people with a legitimate interest in the outcome of the case—called *locus standi*) may ask the Divisional Court to review the case to see whether, eg the court acted judicially, fairly, without bias, observing principles of natural justice, or whether it adopted the correct procedures.

If it did not, the remedy is one or more prerogative orders: *certiorari* to quash a decision; *mandamus* to compel the magistrates' court to act (eg by hearing the case in a proper manner); and *prohibition* to prevent magistrates acting in error. Judicial review must normally be pursued within six months.

Declarations

More rare, are applications to the Divisional Court by either party for that court to declare what the law is on a particular point, or what it means. The magistrates' court then acts on the advice given.

AMENDING SENTENCE/RECTIFYING MISTAKES

- Magistrates' courts have power to correct their own mistakes in certain circumstances. Section 142 of the Magistrates' Courts Act 1980 (as amended) gives them power *inter alia* to amend a sentence if there has been eg:
  —a mistake
  —an unlawful penalty
  —an omission
  or if there are other compelling reasons.
- The power belongs directly to the magistrates and there is, therefore, no right for the offender to make formal application

under section 142; he or she may only ask the magistrates to consider exercising their powers if and as they see fit.

- It is suggested that section 142 should not be used as a general review power or as a response to subsequent changes in circumstances.
- The provision would appear to have been designed to enable the court to make sure that its original sentencing decision was complete and as appropriate as possible based on the facts as they were at the time of its imposition.
- There is, since 1 October 1996:
—no need for the original bench or any member of it to return to act under section 142
—no 28 day limit on the exercise of the power
—power to order a retrial even if the original plea was one of guilty.
- Sensible use of the revised section 142 powers can often avoid unnecessary appeals although advice should always be taken.
  📖 ✍

FREE PARDON

Free pardons are awarded by the Sovereign. This might occur, eg where the normal appeal mechanisms are exhausted or cannot be used, eg because the time limit for an appeal has expired but facts affecting conviction or sentence have now surfaced. A pardon does not remove a conviction; it erases the consequences.

The pace of change in criminal justice matters, and in sentencing in particular, seems unlikely to abate.

Crime (Sentences) Act 1997

The Sentence of the Court incorporates the main changes up until 1 January 1998, including those arising from the Crime (Sentences) Act 1997. Certain other aspects of that Act, *if and when brought into force,* are worth bearing in mind:

- community service orders or curfew orders for fine defaulters
- community service orders or curfew orders instead of a fine in certain circumstances, even if the offence itself is not serious enough to warrant a community sentence
- disqualification from driving for fine defaulters
- disqualification from driving for non-motoring offences
- disclosure of pre-sentence reports (PSRs) to certain prosecutors, seemingly so that they can address the court, for example on areas of fact contained in the report which may contradict statements on the prosecutor's file, or on matters relating to the perspective of the victim.

Crime and Disorder Bill

In 1997, the government introduced a Crime and Disorder Bill. If enacted, this could bring about major changes in the way offenders (especially juveniles, but to a great extent adults also) are sentenced or deterred from criminal or anti-social behaviour. The proposals are expected to be on the statute book by the Spring of 1998, with pilot schemes and phased implementation to follow.[1] Some of the main features which relate specifically, though not necessarily exclusively, to adult offenders include:

- 'anti-social behaviour orders' to prohibit such behaviour, whether or not it might otherwise be possible to prosecute someone for a substantive offence
- 'sex offender orders' to control the actions of convicted sex offenders if they cause concern for public safety

---

[1] Prospective changes which directly address juvenile offending will be considered in a second edition of *Introduction to the Youth Court* (Waterside Press, 1998).

- crime and disorder strategies to link local government and statutory agencies in local measures to combat crime
- direct and radical measures to address delays in the criminal justice system including wide powers of case management for a single justice or justices' clerk
- 'drug treatment and testing orders' to monitor and address medically an offender who is dependent on drugs, especially where the dependency leads to offending
- the establishing by the Lord Chancellor of a National Sentencing Advisory Panel
- a requirement to consider racial aggravation in an offence as a factor which makes it more serious and thus deserving of a higher penalty—with some new, separate racially aggravated versions of existing offences
- early release of short-term prisoners subject to a curfew and electronic monitoring.

Magistrates should seek further advice locally as and when any of the above changes occur. 📖✋

Index

Further introductory books from Waterside Press

Introduction to the Magistrates' Court Bryan Gibson (Third edition scheduled for 1998). A basic outline—plus a *Glossary of Words, Phrases and Abbreviations* (750 entries). An ideal introduction *Law Society Gazette*. A book which many magistrates will wish to carry *The Magistrate*. (1995) ISBN 1 872 870 15 5. £10

Introduction to the Youth Court Winston Gordon, Michael Watkins and Philip Cuddy. **Foreword: Lord Woolf**. Produced under the auspices of the Justices' Clerks' Society. A comprehensive, up-to-date and readable overview *Law Society Gazette*. A must for those interested in the work of the youth courts *The Magistrate*. An extremely useful and practical guide *The Law*. (1996) ISBN 1 872 870 36 8. £12

Introduction to the Family Proceedings Court Elaine Laken, Chris Bazell and Winston Gordon. **Foreword: Sir Stephen Brown**, President of the Family Division of the High Court. Produced under the auspices of the Justices' Clerks' Society. Because of its clarity of information and its lucidity of language and explanation *Introduction to the Family Proceedings Court* is a very accessible handbook *The Magistrate*. (1997) ISBN 1 872 870 46 5. £12

Introduction to Road Traffic Offences Winston Gordon, Philip Cuddy and Andy Wesson. The fourth handbook in *The Sentence of the Court* series. Produced under the auspices of the Justices' Clerks' Society. (Available from May 1998 onwards) ISBN 1 872 870 51 1. £12

Introduction to the Probation Service Anthony Osler. An overview of work with offenders. Also includes the role of the Court Welfare Service in family matters. (1995) ISBN 1 872 870 19 8. £10

Introduction to the Criminal Justice Process Bryan Gibson and Paul Cavadino. Rarely, if ever, has this complex process been described with such comprehensiveness and clarity *Justice of the Peace* (First reprint, 1997) ISBN 1 872 870 09 0. £12

Other publications with a judicial dimension

📖 Criminal Classes Offenders at School Angela Devlin
If you are in any doubt about the links between poor education, crime and recidivism, read it: Marcel Berlins *The Guardian*. (First reprint, 1997) ISBN 1 872 870 30. £16

📖 Tackling the Tag The Electronic Monitoring of Offenders Dick Whitfield
A comprehensive and balanced guide *Prison Report*. Each court library would benefit from a copy *The Justices' Clerk*. (1997) ISBN 1 872 870 53 8. £16

Interpreters and the Legal Process Joan Colin and Ruth Morris Weighty and immensely readable *Law Society Gazette*. An extremely practical guide *The Law*. A scholarly work with everyday practical messages for all professionals *Wig and Gavel*. (1996) ISBN 1 872 870 28 7. £12

Prisons of Promise Tessa West
Foreword: Sir David Ramsbotham, Chief Inspector of Prisons. Extremely well-researched . . . Should be seriously considered by the home secretary *Justice of the Peace*. Deserves to be made available to every magistrate *The Justices' Clerk*. (1997) ISBN 1 872 870 50 3. £16

I'm Still Standing Bob Turney The autobiography of a dyslexic ex-prisoner, now a probation officer. A truly remarkable book *Prison Writing*. (1997) ISBN 1 872 870 43 0. £12

Justice for Victims and Offenders Martin Wright
An informative addition to the excellent Waterside Press series *Vista*. ISBN 1 872 870 35 X. £16

Deaths of Offenders The Hidden Side of Justice Alison Liebling (Ed.) Examines deaths in police, prison and special hospital custody — including on remand and in court and police cells. Published on behalf of ISTD. (1998) ISBN 1 872 870 61 9. £16

Black Women's Experiences of Criminal Justice Ruth Chigwada-Bailey Highlights some major weaknesses in the system *The Manchester Justice*. Compelling . . . A must for decision-makers in the criminal justice process *The Law*. (1997) ISBN 1 872 870 54 6. £16

Hanging in the Balance Brian Block and John Hostettler
A history of the abolition of capital punishment in Britain. **Foreword: Lord Callaghan.** A masterwork *Justice of the Peace*. (1997) ISBN 1 872 870 47 3. £18

Prison Patter Angela Devlin A dictionary of prison slang. Useful for the custody suite *Police Journal*. (1996) ISBN 1 872 870 41 4. £12

Introduction to the Scottish Children's Panel Alistair Kelly Very interesting reading *The Law*. (1996) ISBN 1 872 870 38 4. £12

Conflict Resolution A Foundation Guide Susan Stewart
Of interest to people who deal with disputes — of whatever kind — including through mediation and alternative dispute resolution procedures. (1998) ISBN 1 872 870 65 1. £12

Introduction to Prisons Nick Flynn *et al*

A brand new addition to the successful Waterside Press handbook series. **Foreword: Lord Hurd.** In association with the Prison Reform Trust. (Summer 1998 onwards) ISBN 1 872 870 37 6. £12

Introduction to Criminology A Basic Guide   Russell

Pond A lay person's guide written with people working in criminal justice particularly in mind. The basic ideas of criminology and their sources. (Summer 1998 onwards) ISBN 1 872 870 42 2. £12

Children Who Kill   Paul Cavadino (Ed.) From the tragic

Mary Bell and Jamie Bulger cases to comparable events world-wide. Highly recommended *The Law*. A rich source of information *BJSW*. (1996) ISBN 1 872 870 29 5. £16

A to Z of Criminal Justice   Paul Cavadino A 'mini-

encyclopaedia' of terms and terminology. (Summer 1998 onwards) ISBN 1 872 870 10 4. £18

Capital Punishment Global Issues and Prospects

Peter Hodgkinson/Andrew Rutherford (Eds.) Deserves to be widely read *Law Quarterly Review*. Fascinating and superbly readable *The Law*. (1996) ISBN 1 872 870 32 5. £18

Criminal Justice and the Pursuit of Decency   Andrew

Rutherford Without people committed to humanising penal practice, criminal justice can so easily sink into apathy and pointless repression *Sunday Telegraph*. (First reprint, 1994) ISBN 1 872 870 21 X. £12

Transforming Criminal Policy Andrew Rutherford

Excellent and highly readable *Vista*. (1996) ISBN 1 872 870 31 7. £16

Domestic Violence and Occupation of the Family

Home   Chris Bazell and Bryan Gibson A key work for family law practitioners. Includes the interface with the Protection from Harassment Act 1997. (May 1998 onwards) ISBN 1 872 870 60 0. £18

Invisible Women What's Wrong With Women's

Prisons?   Angela Devlin Women in prison. (June 1998) ISBN 1 872 870 59 7. £18

Until They Are Seven His Honour John Wroath

A true story. The origins of women's rights to property and children. (Autumn 1998) ISBN 1 872 870 57 0. £16

📖 **Growing Out of Crime** The New Era   Andrew Rutherford The classic and challenging work about young offenders. (Second reprint, 1995) ISBN 1 872 870 06 6. £12.50

📖 **Juvenile Delinquents and Young People in Trouble** Willie McCarney (Ed.) An *international* survey of youth justice. Published in conjunction with the International Association of Juvenile and Family Court Magistrates. I would recommend this edition *The Magistrate*. Contains some extremely interesting findings *The Law*. (1996) ISBN 1 872 870 39 2. £18

📖 **Relational Justice** Repairing the Breach Jonathan Burnside/Nicola Baker **Foreword: Lord Woolf.** As featured in *The Guardian*. (1994) ISBN 1 872 870 22 8. £10

📖 **Paying Back** 20 years of Community Service   Dick Whitfield/David Scott (Eds.) **Foreword: Lord Taylor**, Lord Chief Justice. (1993) ISBN 1 872 870 13 9. £12

📖 **Drinking and Driving** A Decade of Development Jonathan Black
Strongly recommended *Justice of the Peace* (1993) ISBN 1 872 870 12 0. £14

📖 **Punishments of Former Days** Ernest Pettifer
A good read *The Magistrate*. (1992) ISBN 1 872 870 05 8. £9.50

📖 **Drugs and Criminal Policy** Penny Green (Summer 1998 onwards) ISBN 1 872 870 33 3. £18

📖 **Geese Theatre Handbook** Working With Offenders and Youth at Risk Drama therapy for offenders – including exercises and instructions for group work. (Late 1998/early 1999) ISBN 1 872 870 67 8. £16

📖 **Going Straight** Angela Devlin and Bob Turney Interviews with people – some well known – who have 'succeeded' after a life inside or a criminal career. (Late 1998/early 1999) ISBN 1 872 870 66 X. £16

All from: **WATERSIDE PRESS** • DOMUM ROAD • WINCHESTER • SO23 9NN. Tel or fax 01962 855567.
INTERNET:106025.1020@compuserve.com
Direct mail prices quoted. *Please add £1.50 per book p&p to £6 max* (UK only: postage abroad charged at cost)

Announcing the

Magistrates Bench Handbook
A Manual for Lay Magistrates

With a Foreword by the Lord Chancellor

ABOUT THE HANDBOOK

The innovative *Magistrates Bench Handbook* has been devised under the direction of a Project Board comprising representatives of:

- The Judicial Studies Board
- The Magistrates' Association
- The Justices' Clerks' Society
- Legal publishers Waterside Press.

AIMS AND PURPOSES

The handbook seeks to build on existing good practice by providing lay magistrates with a range of materials for training and day-to-day reference purposes. The loose-leaf format makes for ease of updating and allows for the addition of further items, in particular items of local interest (below).

CONTENTS

The materials in the handbook focus upon adult offenders appearing in the ordinary magistrates' court. The sections of the handbook contain the following core materials:

1. Introduction

2. The Sentence of the Court
This loose-leaf version is based on the second edition. Specialist handbooks describing the work of the youth court, family proceedings court and road traffic offences are available in paperback. Future

development may mean that these works (and associated materials) will be made available in a loose-leaf format for inclusion in the binder.

3. Guidelines

All courts use guidelines to assist the process of decision-making. Three key tools affecting sentencing have been reproduced from *The Sentence of the Court* in a new A4 format and are contained in *Section 3* of the *Magistrates Bench Handbook:*

The Magistrates' Association Sentencing Guidelines

For many years, the Magistrates' Association has published *Sentencing Guidelines*. These were revised in 1997. The guidelines cover criminal offences in general and also road traffic offences. Importantly, they contain instructions about how they should be used and a special section headed 'Compensation Orders and Table of Awards'.

National Mode of Trial Guidelines

These guidelines, issued by the Lord Chief Justice in 1990, set out factors which magistrates should consider when deciding whether or not to commit a defendant to the Crown Court *for trial,* ie whether an individual 'either way' offence (such as theft, burglary or causing actual bodily harm) is, or is not, more suitable for trial in the Crown Court rather than in the magistrates' court. This is known as the 'mode of trial' decision, sometimes called 'determining venue'.

Considerations Affecting Decisions Whether or Not to Commit to the Crown Court for Sentence

As described in *Chapter 2* of *The Sentence of the Court,* since 1997, magistrates' courts dealing with an either way offence must first ask the defendant whether he or she intends to plead guilty and if there is an intimation of a guilty plea to decide whether to sentence the defendant themselves or to commit him or her to the Crown Court for sentence. These materials are designed to assist such decisions. They are based upon Court of Appeal rulings and guidance.

4. Decision-making

Judicial decision-making has become increasingly complex. It is well recognised that in relation to all but the most straightforward decisions magistrates should seek legal advice and follow a clear structure which will ensure that all relevant matters (and only relevant matters) are considered, and that this happens in the correct sequence. *Section 4* of the *Magistrates Bench Handbook* entitled *Decision-making* comprises: *Structured Decision-making Charts* issued by the Judicial Studies Board

(JSB) in January 1998; and a 'starter pack' of *Reference Sheets* (which can be adapted or added to locally if courts so choose). The JSB charts are as follows:

1. Case Management
2. Bail or Custody
3. Venue for Either Way Offences
4. Guilty or Not Guilty
5. Sentencing
6. Fine Enforcement.

The handbook also contains the following *Reference Sheets*:

1. Equality of Treatment
2. Maximum Penalties Etc.
3. Penalty Points and Disqualification
4. Order of Proceedings
5. Contempt of Court
6. Costs
7. The Public, The Press and Reporting Restrictions
8. Search Warrants
9. Appeals and Re-opening of Decisions
10. PSD Licensing
11. Words and Jargon
12. Possible Future Sentencing Changes
13. Offenders Below 18 Years of Age
14. Natural Justice.

5. Pronouncements
Many courts have their own pronouncements, ie set forms of words which a court chairman can use when announcing a sentence or other decision of the court. The handbook contains the pronouncements developed by the Avon Magistrates' Courts Service which are unique in the sense that they have been awarded the 'Crystal Mark' of the Plain English Campaign.

6. Local Items
It is fundamental to the concept of the handbook that it can be developed to meet *local* needs. This section can be used for whatever purpose an individual court or local area decides is appropriate. For example, details of the following kind could be considered for inclusion:

- frequently changing items
- those of a purely local nature, eg certain benefit rates, council tax
- average earnings locally in trades, jobs, professions
- penalties under local bye-laws
- statements of preferred practice and protocols vis-à-vis the local probation service
- information about community sentences, and bail or other hostels
- notes on the duty solicitor scheme and other services to the court.

THE 'HELPING HAND' SYMBOL 📖✋

Many of the items dealt with in the *Magistrates Bench Handbook* involve complex legal and judicial considerations which are the province of justices' clerks and other court advisers: see, generally, *The Sentence of the Court, Chapter 11*. As in *The Sentence of the Court*, rather than repeating this warning at points where legal/judicial advice is most likely to be needed, a 'helping hand' symbol is used. Whenever this appears, magistrates should seek advice before making their decision or taking a particular course of action.

UPDATING

One purpose of the loose-leaf format is ease of updating. The materials will be revised on a 'needs' basis. It is anticipated that the main updating will occur every 18 months or so. There is an optional facility to subscribe to updates, details of which are sent to each recipient/ provider.

The *Magistrates Bench Handbook* represents an invaluable resource for anyone concerned with decision-making in magistrates' courts. It is also suitable for use in public libraries and law libraries as a ready explanation of how judicial decisions are made in summary cases.

ISBN 1 872 870 62 7

From:

WATERSIDE PRESS • DOMUM ROAD • WINCHESTER • SO23 9NN
Tel or fax 01962 855567. INTERNET:106025.1020@compuserve.com
Direct mail price £28.50 plus *p&p of £3.50* per copy. UK only: postage abroad charged at cost

MAXIMUM PENALTIES ETC.

Conditional discharge

Up to three years. No statutory minimum period.

Fines

Level 1   £200
Level 2   £500
Level 3   £1,000
Level 4   £2,500
Level 5   £5,000   (As at April 1998)

Community sentences

Probation order Minimum six months; maximum three years. For added requirements, seek advice: 📖✋

Community service order Minimum 40 hours; maximum 240 hours. For consecutive orders, seek advice: 📖✋

Combination order
Probation element: minimum 12 months; maximum 3 years.
Community service element: minimum 40 hours; maximum 100 hours.

Attendance centre order (under 21 years of age only) Minimum 12 hours; maximum 36 hours.[1]

Curfew order Minimum two hours; maximum 12 hours—per day for up to six months. Electronic monitoring may support all or part of the curfew period if available. Take advice locally: 📖✋

Custody (Always 📖✋)

Minimum five days; maximum six months (maximum also depends upon the Act which creates the offence).

Normally, up to 12 months in aggregate if two or more *either way* offences.

---

[1] Different rules apply to: (a) orders for *non-payment of fine*: these can be made in respect of defaulters up to and including *age 24: Chapter 3;* and (b) juveniles*:* see *Introduction to the Youth Court/*📖✋

189

MAXIMUM PENALTIES ETC. (Continued)

Compensation

Up to £5,000 per offence of which the defendant stands convicted (but this can include amounts relating to offences taken into consideration/TICs). Take advice unless straightforward: 📖✋

Maximum Periods in Default of Payment of Fines etc.
Always 📖✋

Up to **£200: 7 days**

exceeding £200 but not over **£500: 14 days**

exceeding £500 but not **£1,000: 28 days**

exceeding £1,000 but not **£2,500: 45 days**

exceeding £2,500 but not **£5,000: 3 months**

exceeding £5,000 but not **£10,000: 6 months**

over **£10,000: 12 months**

(As at April 1998)

All subject to reduction for part payment: 📖✋